HOME REMEDIES

HOME REMEDIES

MARTIN POPS

The University of Massachusetts Press Amherst, 1984

Printed in the United States of America
Library of Congress Cataloging in Publication Data
Pops, Martin.
Home remedies.
Includes bibliographical references and index.
Contents: The American fix — In labyrinths — Charles Olson — [etc.]
1. United States—Popular culture. 2. Postmodernism—United States. I. Title.
NX504.P66 1984 700'.973 84-2647
ISBN 0-87023-448-X
ISBN 0-87023-449-8 (pbk.)

For Patricia

Acknowledgments

I am indebted to the following friends and colleagues for their encouragement and criticism: Alan Spiegel, Carl Dennis, Howard Wolf, Donna Sheinberg, Emanuele Licastro, Joseph Germano, Neil Schmitz, Brian Henderson, Albert Cook, Donald Barthelme, Paul Hogan, and Bill Sylvester. My largest debt is to Robert and Peggy Boyers, Editor-in-Chief and Executive Editor of *Salmagundi*: most of these essays first appeared in their magazine. I have slightly revised "The American Fix" (Fall 1971), "In Labyrinths" (Summer/Fall 1974), "Perpetual Motions" (Summer/Fall 1977), and "The Metamorphosis of Shit" (Spring 1982). "Sleeping Beauty Spurned: Remarks on Modern and Postmodern Dance" is a conflation of "The Rape of Sleeping Beauty" (Winter 1971) and "Some Remarks on Modern and Postmodern Dance" (Fall 1980/Winter 1981), from which much has been deleted and a little added. "Charles Olson: Obeying the Figures of the Present Dance" was originally published in *Modern Poetry Studies* (1971) and is much amended; "The Museum, My Home Away from Home" first appeared in the *Bennington Review* (Summer 1983) and is slightly revised.

I wish to thank the committee of the Julian Park Fund of the State University of New York at Buffalo for helping defray the cost of this project, the purchase of photographs, and the permission to reproduce them.

Contents

Preface

THERE are some home remedies, like sex, about which I do not care to write, and others, like drugs, about which I do not much care. I care even less for such official remedies as politics, therapy, or the church of your choice. I remember Emerson reproving Thoreau for a certain want of ambition: "Fault of this, instead of being the head of American Engineers, he is captain of a huckleberry party." (Thoreau might have taken reproof as praise: he was already an inspector of snowstorms.) Huckleberrying is a fine home remedy and the one thing I may say these essays are about.

I have proceeded, then, in a spirit of play. I remember, as a boy, how fascinated I was by the title of a book my mother was reading: *The Left Hand Is the Dreamer*. Was Theodore Reik, I wondered, a lefty like me? And did his left hand really dream? Mine had sometimes fallen asleep, but, as far as I knew, it had never dreamt. My mother explained Reik's metaphor without explaining away the fascination I have never felt for the right hemisphere of my brain. I wrote *Home Remedies* with my left hand: to amuse and subvert.

I did not realize as I wrote, however, that I had lapsed into sexist usage: the arbitrary "he's" and "him's" which an observant editor called to my attention. I pluralized some of these pronouns, but others, more resistant, I alternated by gender—hence the startling "she" in the second paragraph of the first essay. But when I reread that essay, I noticed something even more startling: that the "she" in the first paragraph (the lady who didn't love God) is like the "he" in the second (Adam after the apple): a comic convenience, a playful fiction. I think of *Home Remedies* as a sequence of playful fictions.

The American Fix

"The poet Frank O'Hara once met de Kooning on the street, the painter said that he had been out 'buying some environment' for a picture; under his arm he had a box of drugstore cotton."—Thomas B. Hess, *Willem de Kooning*

THERE was a lady, wrote C. S. Lewis, who didn't love God and didn't know why. Then, one day, she realized that she had, all unknowingly, identified Him, whom she had always supposed was a substance, with tapioca, a substance she hated and would not eat. In her access of insight she grew no fonder of tapioca, but she began to love God. As one says of food that will not down, she no longer rejected Him.

Unfortunately not all metaphysical tales end so happily: consider, for example, the problem of Adam. The core of his difficulty was the apple stuck in his throat he could neither bring up nor get down. Neurosis is an internalized counter-environment (an Adam's apple); but to internalize a counter-environment is to become a counter-environment in somebody else's environment (hence Adam's Expulsion from Eden). If modern artists are leery of psychoanalysis, it is because they fear that as soon as their neuroses are classified, their counter-environments will be declassified. In our time neurosis is an ideal counter-environment, a truly precious wound, through which to create an art of alienation. In psychoanalysis the analysand brings it up, the past she could never properly digest, in order to get it down; in confession the communicant keeps it down in order to get it out. "I got a good clearing out myself, that time," says a trapper in *The Oregon Trail*, of his confession, "and I reckon that will do for me till I go down to the settlements again." Psychoanalysis is a technic of declassification and wound-binding, and an aid to digestion. Confession is a technic of purgation, which is why most of us go to Purgatory.

Marcel Duchamp finally and self-consciously isolated the modern in modern art; he isolated a pure counter-environment as Koch isolated the anthrax bacillus. For example, Duchamp inverted a urinal and called it a fountain, demonstrating that a counter-environment is an environment turned upside down. He inverted a bottle-rack, called it a "readymade," and stepped outside the history of art. Not for long of course. That monster is like the ostrich in *Moby-Dick*, "of potent digestion [who] gobbles down bullets and gun flints"; Robert Motherwell, for instance, argued that the bottle-rack is more beautiful than any intendedly beautiful object of that year, 1914. We should say of Duchamp what was said less truly of Cézanne: that he was the primitive of a new art. Our Pop painters have refined his procedures, and it is much harder to accuse them of making an inadvertently beautiful object. It is hard making a case for the vinyl hamburger and the plaster-of-paris pie, the coke bottles and the beer cans, the apples and the spaghetti, the meat cases and the pastry cases, the hot dogs and the chili, the candycane and the Spam, the Campbell Soup and the Velveeta Cheese, the submarines and the Seven-Up. It is hard making a case for the kind of art Claes Oldenburg says he is for: "U.S. Government Inspected Art, Grade A art, Regular Price art, Yellow Ripe art, Extra Fancy art, Ready-to-eat art, Best-for-less art, Ready-to-cook art, Fully cleaned art, Spend Less art, Eat Better art, Ham art, pork art, chicken art, tomato art, banana art, apple art, turkey art, cake art, cookie art."[1] This is an art pretty hard for any ostrich to swallow.

Saliva in the mouth is easy to swallow. But if you spit it into a glass and then, as Edmund Carpenter suggests, try to drink it . . . why, it becomes a gun flint. "Everything the artist spits is art," said Kurt Schwitters, the greatest of junk collagists.[2] Norman Mailer tells of a women's liberation test: drink your menstrual blood. Some of my students, unprepared for the random movement of the Ann Halprin dance company, were, in their word, nauseated. If they didn't throw up, it was because they swallowed their anxiety. On seeing Picasso's *Demoiselles d'Avignon*, the first Cubist painting, Braque said: "It is as though we were supposed to exchange our usual diet for one of tow and paraffin."[3] There is, in fact, in the foreground of the painting a spiky still life on which one could not fail to choke. Gorges still rise on seeing Meret Oppenheim's *Fur-covered Tea-cup, Spoon, and Saucer*; like Duchamp's *Fountain*, it is—as one commonly says of art one finds offensive—disgusting, in bad taste. Goya kept his monstrous painting of *Saturn Devouring His Children* in his dining room. Robert Indiana, author of the hard-edge Pop injunction *EAT*, said of Abstract Expressionist paint-handling, "Impasto is visual indigestion."[4]

E. H. Gombrich has remarked the relation between the language of art criticism and that of the cuisine; food is the world about which we first begin to exercise judgment, discrimination, and taste. Separated from the breast, we experience doubleness, a separation from ourselves, the phantom ache of amputation. In *The American Scene* Henry James poignantly records the razing of his "birth-house" and the erection of skyscrapers which now block his "view of the past, that the effect for me, in Washington Place, was of having been amputated of half my history." We are, in this sense, all amputees. Symptom formation confirms Original Sickness as symbol formation augurs the art that temporality reconstitutes. The drug addict is a literalist of the imagination who settles for psychic dissolution, who reconstitutes the uroboric round by shooting into his arm. Putting one's foot in one's mouth, literally or figuratively, also creates a metaphoric uroboros: the confining and recycling of energy inside the self. So does masturbating. A drug—penicillin, aspirin, heroin—is a counter-environment that dissolves a counter-environment. That is why, with life at stake, such drugs are called "wonder" or "miracle" drugs—after our archetypal curatives for spiritual deadness, the wine and the wafer. But if we were truly wonderworking, we could expel the apple as God expelled Adam.

"Art," said Duchamp, "is a habit-forming drug,"[5] and we have inured ourselves to its shock as an addict inures herself to a higher dose. The double bind of modern art, like the double bind of modern civilization, traps us between Death and Life-in-Death. Les Levine asks us to link hands in an event he calls *Shock Treatment*. Only connect—though the weak voltage that courses through us is a Gothic *frisson*, not a shock of recognition. A stronger dose would kill the patient anesthetized. Andy Warhol silk-screened the *Electric Chair*, but Life-in-Death has really won us all. And that means a diet of cold turkey, though now—after a hundred years—we have finally developed a taste for avant-garde art, for counter-environments. Perhaps I should say we have developed a craving, as if art, like any other consumer product, were subject to fashion and newfanglednesse. I think of Max Ernst's witty etchings of 1920, *Not Art but Fashion*. What can a poor artist do if he cannot create an object unique in its indigestibility? He can, with Warhol, quantify an object endlessly: Brillo boxes, for example ("life-size," as the catalogues say), indistinguishable from the commercial product. What are they then, accidents or essences, and how can you tell? Well, what are the wine and the wafer? If a transubstantiation occurs, it is because the artist is a magician who has convinced us despite the evidence of our senses. And people do buy Brillo boxes. Art and Life have never been more virtually congruent.

Warhol incarnates the counter-environment of the apparently homosexual other, the outrage of repetition (cf. Gertrude Stein) where Camp and Campbell Soup cross. Warhol once did work in fashion advertising but gave it up because, as he said, it was too hard being creative; now he creates works as if he were a machine and says, "I think everybody should be a machine." It's much easier "because you do the same thing every time."[6] Whitman, whose errors are prizes of Camp extravagance, thought he could turn and live with animals because "they are so placid and self-contained" and, like Warhol's machines, do not suffer human anguish.

To exhibit Brillo boxes is to confer aesthetic status on them, automatically. Duchamp exhibited the readymades only once (in

1916) and he exhibited his "rotoreliefs"—startling anticipations of Op Art—not in a gallery but in a gadget show. To confer status upon a readymade (even to multiply it in great number) is to violate the anartistic object's being-in-anonymity. So on signing replicas of the readymades, Duchamp reasonably observed, "I like signing all those things—it *devalues* them."[7] Understandably, he left his masterpiece *The Bride Stripped Bare by Her Bachelors, Even*, definitively unfinished. Advertising makes bullets and gun flints readily digestible. To advertise a readymade would have meant sacrificing its freedom and conceding its identity; the same is true of advertising the self. Duchamp never did either.

One can quantify but one can also destroy unique objects, as Jean Tinguely has done in his self-destroying contraption appropriately entitled *Homage to New York*, but best of all, as in Conceptual art, one can exhibit documentary evidence that certain objects once existed or still exist in the mind of the artist but are, in any event, physically unavailable. And then what can a poor bourgeois do to feed his collecting mania? Wring his hands in frustration, like a parent whose child has been arrested for drugs, and say, "Where did we go wrong?" In 1918 Duchamp declared the *Corkscrew Shadow* an immaterial work of art. In Abstract Expressionism the painting is a shadow of an act that is a substance, but in Conceptual art even the painting has retreated into the world of Forms. The art work has never been purer or more undefiled.

If the environment can assimilate the counter-environment, the counter-environment can also assimilate the environment. Claes Oldenburg once said of New York City: "I saw street refuse as elaborate accidental compositions."[8] I am not speaking now of Richard Stankeiwicz's junk sculpture nor even of Robert Morris's "scatter pieces" and random piles. I am speaking, for example, of the photographs dutifully collected in Peter Blake's book about the shame of America, *God's Own Junkyard*, photographs which are supposed to infect us with remorse but which in fact, ironically reveal the aesthetic potentialities of pure refuse. With luck the empedestalized beer can will rediscover its place on the highway.

There is a sculpture by Marisol called *Love* in which a Coca-

Cola bottle is crammed down the throat of a masklike, sexually indeterminate, face. In a consumer culture Everyman eats it, Everyman sucks. In *The Pause That Refreshes* Mel Ramos painted a nude of luscious breasts standing half-concealed behind a sign advertising Coca-Cola, the very milk and pap of American life. Ramos has also painted an odalisque reclining atop a package of cheese and a nude emergent from a banana. Pop Art, says Roy Lichtenstein, "*is* an involvement with what I think to be the most brazen and threatening characteristics of our culture, things we hate, but which are also powerful in their impingement on us."[9] The icons of Pop Art, in other words, exude a negative fascination and veer often enough, as in Marisol and Ramos, toward the pornographic, the alienation of the sexual self. Near the hard-core one could locate Joe Tilson's *Clip-o-matic Lips*, a photographic image of opened, red, brazen lips, or the painting by another Englishman, Peter Phillips's *Star/Card/Table*, for another opened brazen mouth eager to suck. Though not rendered pornographically, James Rosenquist's *Marilyn Monroe* and Tom Wesselman's *Smoker* both depict disembodied lascivious mouths and sharklike teeth as of the *vagina dentata*, eager to castrate. Toward the soft core we find the cinema and silk screens of that oral fantast, Andy Warhol: his films, *Kiss, Eat, Mario Banana*, and *Blow Job* (a sound version of which is called *Eating Too Fast*),[10] and his large two-panel piece called *Marilyn Monroe's Lips*, which consists of 168 images of Marilyn's lips and teeth. Another silk screen of her—Warhol has done at least seven different ones—is called *The Six Marilyns*, subtitled *Marilyn Six Pack*. If we identify eating and sucking with their original object, the mother's milky breast in the world of unamputated wholeness, then it is reasonable to conclude that the images of mechanical food and drink are subtly blasphemous, that the chromed vegetables are the counterparts of pornographic desire.

A punch to the jaw may well awaken the groggy prizefighter. Pornography, like the comic strip (Nathanael West, Roy Lichtenstein), science fiction (William Burroughs, Eduardo Paolozzi), and the fairy tale (Donald Barthelme, Jim Dine), arouses the anesthetized perceiver—it is the counter-environment of kitsch newly impressed into the art of the museums. In an image constellated of sex, drugs, and food, Tristan Tzara announced the social achievement of Dada in 1921: "Dada has inserted its syringe into hot bread."[11] Native American Pop artists simply do not traffic in fetishism or the lurid sexuality of such original Europeans as Richard Lindner, Tomi Ungerer, Allen Jones, and Marcel Duchamp (in his latest work). We are quite innocent in comparison, more infantile, more homoerotic: in fact we seem not to have escaped the homoerotic ambiance of our culture explored by D. H. Lawrence and Leslie Fiedler. The dream of ingestion lies deeper than the daydream of coition. Let Tom Wesselman's *Great American Nude* series of languid women—their vulvas, nipples, and mouths prominently exposed and accentuated—represent our regressive daydream. With few exceptions American Pop is not an art of social protest—there can be no social protest when the counter-environment is finally the environment. In fact, the work of an artist like Warhol bespeaks a spectacular detachment, the numbing of Duchamp's "irony of affirmation" into a put-on, a passive and voyeuristic acceptance. Or as Jim Dine said: "It seems the most natural thing in the world to have that fur-lined teacup."[12]

2 In 1920 Duchamp decided to become the other of Rimbaud's famous allegation, "*I* is another."[13] What, then, is most antithetical to a French Catholic avant-garde painter of bourgeois lineage? "I first wanted to get a Jewish name, but I didn't find one. Then the idea jumped at me, why not a female name? Marvelous! Much better than to change religion would be to change sex. Rose was the most corny name for a girl at that time in French, and Sélavy, of course, was *C'est la vie*. . . . It was a sort of readymadeish action."[14] Man Ray photographed Duchamp as the glamorous Rrose (*sic*: i.e., Eros) and Rrose Sélavy created many objects. A more impressive readymadeish gesture was to give up painting altogether—which Duchamp did in 1923, becoming a chess master instead. We have all since learned, from other sources of course, that easel-painting is dead, but in the Museum Without

Walls, one finds the Duchamp in a place of honor. In 1958, Duchamp constructed a *Self-portrait* by tearing a piece of paper until what remained formed his profile. We recognize him and his works in the silhouette of their nonexistence. Duchamp assumed his last identity in 1954 in the days of proto-Pop, an identity more wondrous and exotic than any of the others: he became an American citizen. Subsequently he told Pierre Cabanne that he had not been to the Louvre in twenty years.[15] Profoundly skeptical of received art, he had become more American than the Americans.

Henry James became a British citizen in 1915 and everyone knows why: in America there were no forms, no tradition, no society, no sense of the past, no sacred fount. No art could come of such sociocultural impoverishment, etc., etc. James's exemplum "The Real Thing" definitively argues that the real thing can never be art. James died in 1916 and Dada was born in Zürich the same year, though Duchamp, on behalf of the future, had already fastened a bicycle wheel onto a stool. Instead of James's endless judgment, discrimination, and taste, Duchamp claimed that his choice of readymade objects "was based on a reaction of *visual* indifference with at the same time a total absence of good or bad taste . . . in fact a complete anesthesia."[16] For the American Henry James, as for Irving, Cooper, Hawthorne, and Adams, the past is the temporal counter-environment of the beleaguered present. Civilization is a jeopardized enclave, and beyond its walls James sees the ominous encroachment, the random jumble, of the New York City skyline, which, in the passion of his fear and disgust, he compares with a jagged comb. In 1915 Duchamp visited New York City for the first time, perceived cosmos not chaos, organic extension not encroachment, inclusivity not isolation: "New York itself is a work of art, a complete work of art. Its growth is harmonious, like the growth of ripples that come on the water when a stone has been thrown into it."[17] In 1916 Duchamp offered a gray steel comb as a readymade.

In 1923 he designed a *Wanted* poster featuring two photographs of himself as an American criminal, George W. Welch, alias Bull, alias Pickens, alias Rrose Sélavy. "Operated Bucket

Shop in New York under name HOOKE, LYON, and CINQUER." Duchamp's poster was premature but prophetic: he was not wanted by American art (except in isolated instances) until the generation of Jasper Johns and Robert Rauschenberg. Though he originally and ironically praised us for our plumbing and bridges (after all he had overturned an *American* urinal), he wanted us right from the start. From his point of view we were singularly blessed:

> In Europe the young always act as the grandsons of some great man—Victor Hugo, or Shakespeare, or someone like that. Even the Cubists liked to say they were grandsons of Poussin. They can't help it. And so when they come to produce something of their own the tradition is indestructible. They're up against all those centuries and all those miserable frescoes which no one can even see any more—we love them for their cracks. That doesn't exist here [in America]. You don't give a damn about Shakespeare, do you? You're not his grandsons at all. So it's a good terrain for new developments. There's more freedom here, less [*sic*] remnants of the past among young artists. They can skip all that tradition, more or less, and go more quickly to the real.[18]

America's first art of the real was Abstract Expressionist painting, created by a group of men—among them, Pollock, Kline, de Kooning, Rothko—who were specialists in urban alienation. Our second art of the real was Pop. As the *Wanted* poster indicates, Duchamp, like Gide and Godard, was stimulated by American gangsterism, our mythological life of the real, though only Duchamp and American art eventually swallowed one another hook, line, and sinker. This is still the country where you buy environment in a drugstore.

The experienced museum-goer mindlessly passes the same Kandinsky a hundred times murmuring, "There's the Kandinsky. Goodbye Kandinsky!" The occasional museum-goer paused before the *Mona Lisa* (on loan from the Louvre to the Metropolitan some years ago) for an average of thirteen seconds. In any event, contemplation of a work of art in a museum can hardly be a private experience in the age of Acousti-guide and those mass audiences that invariably infringe upon the consciousness of a single person silently viewing a single work. In 1968 Duchamp died and his final project, *Etant Donnés* or *Given: 1. The Waterfall/ 2. The Illuminating Gas* (1946–1966), was posthumously installed at the Philadelphia Museum of Art. At his request it became available for viewing only after he had taken permanent residence in the Future. In an age of enormous paintings, Duchamp forces the spectator to look through two peepholes in a wooden door if he would see what lies beyond. Art as religion was never as good as God anyway, says Duchamp, and those peepholes in the door comically restore our one-to-one relation with Art, as if in blasphemy of the confessional.

The scene within, a "sculpture-construction," is quite, quite shocking, and it is impossible to retain an absolute equanimity. Eyes at the door, you discover that you have become a voyeur, that you are having a private experience in a public place. Like a readymade, you have been inverted. You have become an anxious object. Photographs are forbidden not because of the scandalousness of the subject but because reproductions prepare us to not experience originals. Do we prefer Leonardo's *Mona Lisa* or Duchamp's? John Cage expressed his appreciation of the latter by saying: once we had only the *Mona Lisa*, now we have her with a mustache. And Andy Warhol, who frequently does silk screens of the stars (e.g., Elizabeth Taylor, Jacqueline Kennedy) has done several *Mona Lisas*, one of which includes thirty images of her. With Cagean logic, it is entitled *Thirty Are Better Than One*. Duchamp's version *LHOOQ* is an abbreviation for "*Elle a chaud au cul*," and that, implies Duchamp, is the reason for her smile. The mustache and goatee, drawn carefully in pencil, suggest Leonardo's homosexuality. Do we prefer Freud's Leonardo or Duchamp's?

In 1965 Duchamp designed an invitation in the center of which he printed a copy of Leonardo's portrait; the card is entitled *LHOOQ Shaved*. So Mona Lisa is first defaced and then stripped bare by her bachelor, and beyond the garden door lies a ravished, partially dismembered nude, her vulva shaved: the body of Renaissance art in the violated sanctuary of her counter-environment.

3 Ringling Brothers, Barnum and Bailey no longer displays the fattest lady in the world (except in papier mâché) nor the thinnest man (save on stilts), nor albinos, nor mutants. It has two midgets but one amiably acknowledges the other is shorter. I could go on but the point is clear; the circus is not a sinister other anymore. The circus should be about Slavs and Serbo-Croats and the Wild Man of Borneo, Picasso's *Saltimbanques*, Browning's *Freaks*, and Andreyev's *He Who Gets Slapped*, but instead it is about black basketballers on unicycles and nets under the high-wire walkers. The fix is in.

The carnival is a little riskier. There is the fun house and the Ferris wheel, and they correspond to the two primary and alternate modes of American exploration. The fun house is full of spooks and distorted reflections of the self, a metaphoric descent into the constantly surprising realm of the unconscious, the world as embodied in the quasi-religious sea adventure of *Moby-Dick* (1851) where the distorted reflection of Ishmael's ego is the accompanying dark man, Queequeg. The Ferris wheel is full of outward dangers, a challenge directed toward the natural world as embodied in the land adventure of *The Oregon Trail* (1849); Parkman's companion, of course, is white and, unlike Ishmael, Parkman learns nothing of his interior self though much about American geography. The model of the fun house and *Moby-Dick* correspond to the hippie's hallucinatory drug trip; the model of the Ferris wheel and *The Oregon Trail* corresponds to the astronauts' trip to the moon. (In terms of popular films the distinction is between Science Fiction and the Western.) The acid taker supposedly trips with his guru, his wise other; the astronaut is accompanied by another astronaut who is his fraternal twin. In Mailer's terms this division in America's psychic life is between hip and square, and their relationship is that of ego-consciousness to its shadowy underside. In fact, the languages of the drug trip and the moon trip are synonymous. The drug taker is in his *pad*; he takes LSD and experiences a *blast*, then a *taking-off* and a *going-up*. He leaves *ground control* behind, which may *bring* him *down* if he seems to be in trouble. Otherwise he is *taking a trip*; he is *high, flying, coasting, floating, spaced*, and *spaced-out*, though his goal is described as "inner space" not outer. Depending upon how well his system is functioning, he either *comes down* or is *talked down*. He *re-enters* normative space and (again depending upon how well his system is functioning) he either *lands* or *crashes*.[19]

The addict and the astronaut are brothers under the skin. One takes heroin, the other is proclaimed a hero, and in fact *heroin* and *hero* derive from the same Greek word. In the jargon of drug taking, one's first shot of heroin is called one's *wings*. America, are you feeling depressed after the mullahs and ayatollahs? Take a ride on the Space Shuttle. Satisfaction guaranteed (for a day or two). If religion is the opiate of the people, LSD is the religion of the hip people and the space program is the religion of the square. Life in outer space is the Great American Fix.

The first thing to notice about our missiles is the number of them named after Greek gods: Apollo, Saturn, Mercury, Gemini, Jupiter, Poseidon, and so on. We do not name them after our own gods—Christ, Mary, Jehovah (in a more ecumenical spirit)—not merely because we dare not insult the myths of our culture, not merely because Greek names are traditional for astral bodies, but because we are whoring after strange gods with a reputation for power (as we name prophylactics after legendarily potent Semites and Trojans). We are not at all certain of our own powers of ascension, and the type of our naming is the index of cultural failure. If the Christ missile collapsed on the pad, wouldn't that confirm our worst suspicions?

The moon missile itself is an anonymously made icon of worship, like Chartres. The decision to outdo the paynim Russians, the mobilization of national skills and resources, the invention of new engineering procedures, remind me of nothing so much as the religious fervor, the cathedral-building Mariolotry of the Middle Ages. Sending a man to the moon by the end of the sixties in response to President Kennedy's exhortation was like initiating a pilgrimage to the Holy Land on the Celestial Railroad, an ironic tract in the mythos of deliverance. But, as Thoreau observed, "there is more religion in men's science than there is science in their religion." How different is Lyell's deep geologic time from Melville's, whose White Whale is also antemosaic?

Technicians prepare for the firing of a missile by a check-off system called a countdown, and it is of particular interest that the system is not called a countup or countacross. The missile lifts off only at the moment of zero time, that moment, in the language of Mircea Eliade, when profane time is obliterated and man enters the mythological present, the time of timelessness, the sacred time of primitivity. Similarly, the missile is always launched from an area prohibited the casual observer, the altarlike launching pad, for an unprofaned space is as necessary to the success of the enterprise as an unprofaned time. I have noted the analogy of blast (or flash) with drugs; I might note it now with sex. From the pad (slang for bed) an aerodynamically designed missile erects an astronaut who himself personifies a body phallus. Of course the collocation of the sacred and the sexual is a natural phenomenon in the religious experience of primitive man; modern (American) man would reprimitivize his experience in order to resacralize his life, to recyclize time and escape "the terror of history." The missile is shot from land by fire into air and is sometimes recovered in water; the elements which truly count are neither those discovered in nature nor made in the laboratory but those which reaffirm an elemental experience of the world.

In space the astronaut experiences the sensation of weightlessness (as the addict does under the influence of heroin); in fact, Ed White "walked in space" and didn't want to return to the capsule. He was attached by an umbilical lifeline and, floating free, experienced the weightlessness of the fetus in the womb. He had become a child again—no wonder he didn't want to rejoin the fallen world of men.

Apollo is the name of our moon program, and we like to think we are guided by the god of light, reason, and consciousness. But we are no better than Ancient Mariners—"In his loneliness and fixedness he yearneth toward the journeying moon"—and we shall not end as well. In his double bind the Ancient Mariner, struck by the sun, is miraculously rescued by the moon, by Mary, Queen of Heaven. We deny dread as the Ancient Mariner denied the dreadful sea-beasts—death by suffocation on the lunar surface, said one of our astronauts, is just another "contingency"—and we send our ambassadors under the sign of light to the Eternal Feminine, the archetypal other whose darker side we have never seen. We seek a union of Apollo and Luna, a *coincidentia oppositorum*, to heal the blight of Protestant consciousness. The structure of our action is romantic and primitivist, a quest for the sacred not in but through technology, but even this knowledge is too fearful for us to know. We become sentimental and domesticate our passion in an exhausted form. Astronauts have read from Genesis, and a stamp was printed with the words "In the Beginning God." Vice-President Agnew reported how the earth shook at blast-off, and President Nixon declared the week of America's moon shot the most important in the history of the world since the Creation. This little piggie played golf; this little piggie stayed home; this little piggie had a hot pastrami sandwich; this little piggie had none. The private fixes of art, drugs, and sex are converted into the public ones of religion and technology—fixes, we might say, of redeeming social importance.

We seek gods of divine power for protection in a just cause: Apollo, Mercury, Saturn. But we make a pact with darkness when we suspect the gods of light cannot help us. Thus we named our helicopters in Vietnam after Indians and snakes—the Cayuse, the Chinook, the Iroquois (which means "real adders"), and the Cobra. For a similar reason demonic Ahab commands the *Pequod*, named for an extinct but once warlike Indian tribe. In terms of personal bravery, professional competence, incredible expenditure, and technological complexity, one can argue that whaling was the mid-nineteenth-century American version of rocketry. In terms of *Moby-Dick* there are certain other suggestive details: as the astronauts are quarantined and maintained on a special diet before blast-off in order to insure their physical health, Queequeg undergoes his Ramadan of fasting and solitude in order to insure his psychic health; as the missile is launched in sacred time, the *Pequod* embarks on Christmas day. But the astronauts are all Starbucks: they make voyages of commerce not conquest. There is no dread aboard the Apollo because the psychiatrists have weeded the Ahabs out of the program. Ahab would possess the moon by taking off his space helmet, an unforeseen "contingency," even as he dies strangled umbilically against the Great Mother he can never overcome. But his death, as we know, releases Ishmael from dread into rebirth in the maternal sea. For him whom it is written "ye shall be as gods," that man may pass through all the way-stages of psychic development in genius, in courage, in luck. He too may reconstitute an original wholeness not, like the addict, in psychic dissolution but in transcendence. But how can we be reborn if death is just another "contingency"?

How many pilgrimages can we make to the Heavenly City, that airless satellite, fitting symbol of our wisdom and our woe? The problem remains and deepens: how to create an existential space, outer or inner, how to widen the margin so the flesh does not choke, how to resist a suffocation in being? The two most visible "solutions" of the sixties were provided by those spectres at the psychic edge: the hippie and the militarist. For the hippie the way free was through drugs, hair, and clothes—the beatnikery of the fifties exacerbated. Drugs widen the margin because they extend the boundaries of the psychic being; hair widens the margin because it literally extends the boundaries of the physical being. As collage restores three-dimensionality to a two-dimensional plane, drugs and hair restore "dimensionality" to one-dimensional man. Dress becomes a multisensory experience in textures, sounds, colors, and spaces: gallon hats, cowboy boots, colored glasses, studded jackets, love beads, wide belts, pouches, patches, flags, stains, hair, and dirt. Their purpose is to hapticize the physical self, create a tactile existence, sensualize occupied space. In an industrial culture one becomes a hand-made, pre- or anti-industrial artifact, an assemblage of haptic interplay. In truth, though the derivation was not conscious, hippie style devolves from Abstract Expressionist and "stain" painting—works of controlled accident, flamboyant, visceral, deep-dyed, enactive, projecting an existential space and scale in the act of painting.

The militarist in the sixties (and half the seventies) had Vietnam—the defense of Korea exacerbated. In the division of the world into self and other—to rework George Kennan's theory of the "containment" of Communism—Vietnam became the boundary of the self we had to defend for fear that if we didn't, the self (and the physical space we had identified with it) would be contaminated. Needless to say, if we hadn't defined the boundary, we wouldn't have had to defend what we used to call the perimeter of the free world. The domino theory works best with dominoes. The boundary between self and other which the hippie in his person is eager to erase, the militarist is eager to consolidate. To amend a once-fashionable formula of R. D. Laing: the hippie fears a petrifaction of the self, the militarist an implosion, and the rest of us who are a little anxious about either or both can take some comfort in vitamin C. Those of us who secretly wish to affirm boundaries will take vitamin C because it renders the self invulnerable to the virus of subversion from within and invasion from without. So says Linus Pauling, Nobel Prize winner for chemistry. Those of us who secretly wish to deny boundaries will take it because, in rendering the self invulnerable, it allows for peaceful coexistence in the body politic, for the risk and achievement of a fuller life. So says Linus Pauling, Nobel Prize winner for peace.

And beyond vitamin C there is ecology and jogging. Free that space around our bodies, we say, and free our bodies in that space. But the space around us has been dying ever since the seventeenth century, and the wall Captain Ahab said was shoved near to him is the wall we are all up against. Enclosed in shrinking counter-environments, we suffer an ontological suffocation pure air—hyperventilated or not—cannot assuage. Restore the environment, we say, and restore us to it. But can we ever succeed? We might solicit the opinion of that master environmentalist, Marcel Duchamp. In 1919 he chose a sealed-glass ampoule as a readymade, entitled it *Paris Air*, and brought it to the United States. The ampoule contained fifty cc. of Parisian air—hence its title—and in America it constituted a pure and unpolluted counter-environment. Eventually, of course, and predictably, it broke.

In Labyrinths

EDGAR ALLAN POE wrote "The Raven" (if we may believe his arch account) as if he were a detective solving a crime, as if he had come to realize that fiction is a series of clues in search of a solution. If "the job of the detective is to restore [the community to a] state of grace,"[1] then Jehovah was our first detective. He staked out Adam, questioned the suspect, extracted a confession, and restored the garden. Adam hid behind some trees, but God hid behind a two-way mirror. Nowadays only detectives (i.e., psychologists) hide behind two-way mirrors. The detective story is a kind of wisdom literature.

M. Dupin is a wiseman, which means he possesses the faculties of Imagination and Fancy. As we meet him in "The Purloined Letter" he is at once a poet ("I have been guilty of certain doggerel myself") and an adept at mathematical logic, though he scorns the skill.[2] He is a fit rival for the thieving Minister D—— who is also poet and mathematician: like God and Lucifer, they are reciprocals of one another in a primitive universe. "As poet *and* mathematician," Dupin explains, "he [D——] would reason well; as mere mathematician, he could not have reasoned at all, and thus would have been at the mercy of the Prefect" (219). The Prefect of Police cannot solve the crime because he is not a poet, not creative. He is trapped by microscopes and measurements, fixities and definites. He is an instance of the failure of unchecked Fancy as

Henry James's investigator in *The Sacred Fount* is an instance of the failure of unchecked Imagination. This man, who means to determine the precise sexual intertwining of his acquaintances, insists on confining himself to "psychologic evidence."[3] "What's ignoble," he says, "is the detective and the keyhole" (52). Wiretapping is dirty business, said Justice Holmes—and Sherlock would have agreed—but to confine oneself solely to the evidence of untested and uncontested theory is to remain as ignorant, finally, as Poe's untheorizing Prefect. To confine oneself in such a manner is to risk the accusation of madness. *The Sacred Fount* is a demonstration of how consciousness, at its own peril, creates its own reality.

Children learn to throw protective walls around themselves, "defenses" (as the psychologists say) against a threatening world. At the age of six, James's Maisie discovered "a new feeling, the feeling of danger; on which a new remedy rose to meet it, the idea of an inner self or, in other words, of concealment. . . . She would forget everything, she would repeat nothing, and when, as a tribute to the successful application of her system, she began to be called a little idiot, she tasted a pleasure new and keen."[4] Maisie becomes mazy and she knows it. She practices concealment for pleasure and physic. She founds an inner self as men founded cities in the ancient world. When Ascanius was surrounding Alba Longa with walls, he performed a maze-dance on horseback of

1 A neolithic rock carving

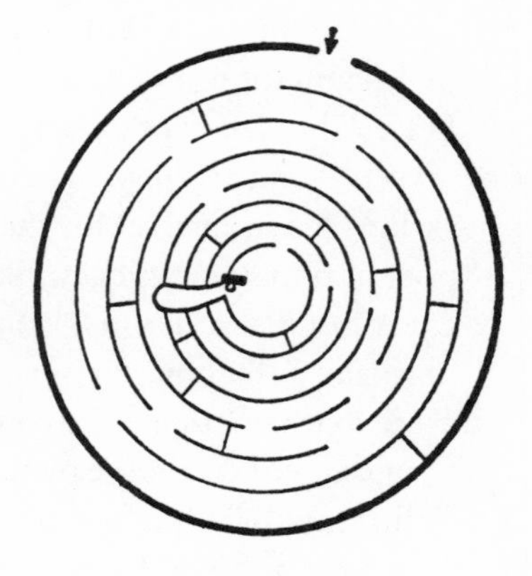

2 A modern cartoon

such indeterminate complexity that Vergil compared it with the Cretan labyrinth. Ascanius intended to weave an entanglement around his city his enemies could never undo.[5] As naturally as a spider spins a web, man extrudes a maze out of and around himself.

Maisie learns the choreography of behavior, the maze-dance of dissimulation. Dupin and D—— turn life into a dance. The structure of "The Purloined Letter" is like a child's puzzle of identically bent nails.

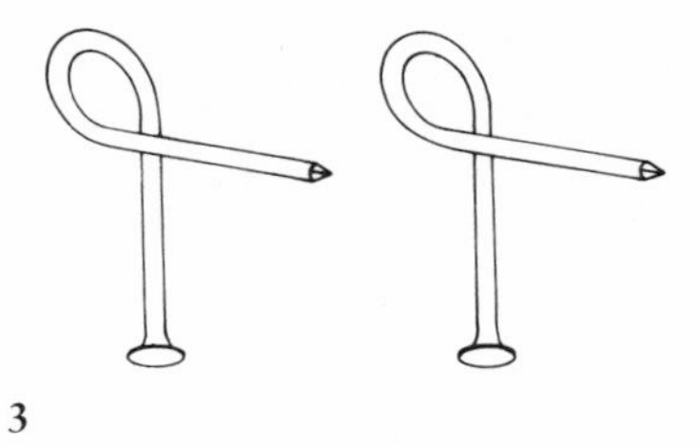

3

D—— entangles the nails.

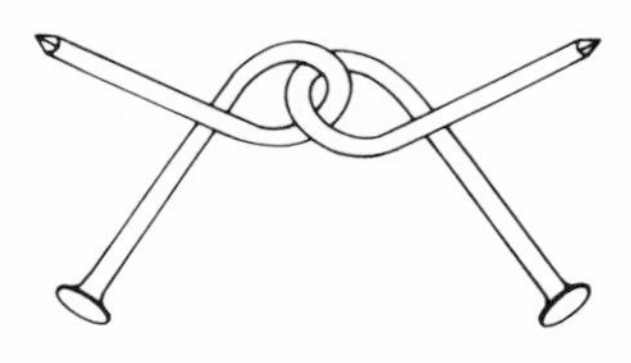

4

That is, he steals a precious letter by substituting a worthless double. Now a solution is wanted but force is not allowed: fair play demands that Dupin not murder D—— to prevent him from blackmail. Dupin solves the puzzle as if he were disentangling the nails: that is, he steals back the precious letter by substituting a worthless double. As D——'s double, Dupin symmetrically reverses what D—— has done.

D—— once did Dupin "an evil turn" (225) in Vienna; now Dupin does D—— an evil turn in Paris. Although Dupin assures us that D—— will be politically destroyed for his wickedness, we suspect his career is not over. In fact, Dupin purposely leaves a "clue" (225) so that D—— will know who has reversed him. What happened in the past and happens in the present will happen in the future. D—— and Dupin are themselves bent nails who, in sword dances of challenge and response, entangle and disentangle their lives. And now it is D——'s turn again.

D—— and Dupin are collaborators who make crime as if it were art. Although Poe assigns them moral valences—Dupin calls D—— a "monstrum horrendum" (224)—we do not locate their crime solely in a moral context, and we hardly remember the Minister's anticipated fall from grace. We locate their crime in an aesthetic context, and its symmetry delights us. Poe enacts the puzzle through his tale which he represents in his tale. Detective fiction, as Poe knew, is written looking backward.

At the end of "The Purloined Letter," D—— has not yet discovered that Dupin has reversed him. For D—— there has been no reversal. For Dupin there has been a reversal. For the reader, the hiatus between Dupin's action and D——'s passion will be a time of fullness in which the bent nails are simultaneously entangled and disentangled in the posture of a pas de deux.

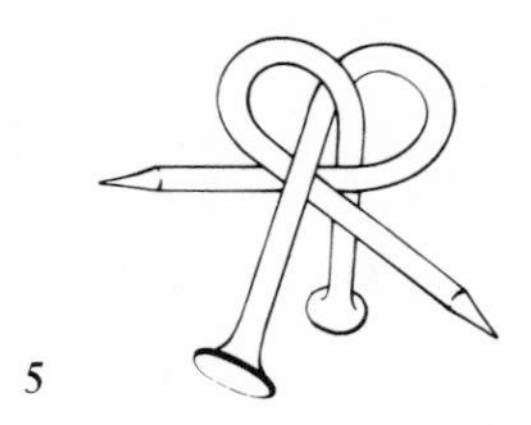

5

"We have Art," said Nietzsche, "in order that we may not perish from Truth," but the opposite danger is that Art (or any artifice) may exclude us from Truth. Consider the neurotic stonemasonry of James's Fleda Vetch who erects "a high wall . . . [a] great false front" only to discover that by denying the world an intercourse with her, she denies herself an intercourse with the world.[6] Or consider the paranoid passion of Kafka's mole who builds, guards, and repairs an immense labyrinth against nameless terrors. As we extrude a labyrinth in order to protect ourselves, we must master the labyrinth we extrude in order to protect ourselves. We must master a dialectic of spaces, and we may have to go far and wee in order to do that. *The Narrative of Arthur Gordon Pym* carried Poe out of space and out of time.

Pym experiences three chasms near the South Pole as an interconnecting labyrinth, "graven . . . within the hills" by God Himself at Creation.

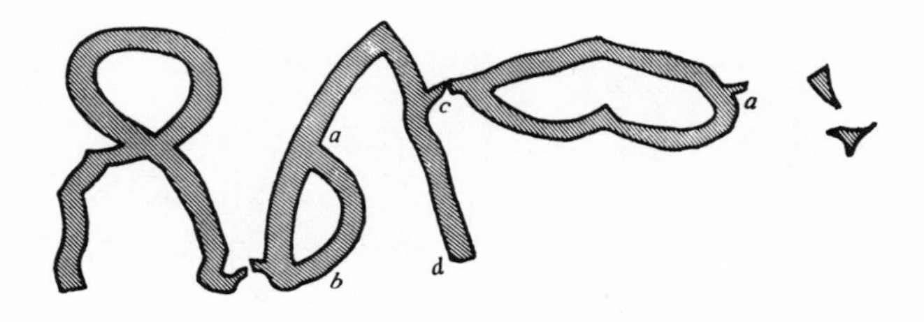

6 I have connected the chasms Poe drew separately.

Though Pym does not know it, they resemble the "Ethiopian verbal root . . . ጸለመ፡ 'To be shady'—whence all the inflections of shadow or darkness" (197)—and, rather more vaguely, the English letters eap.[7] Rock inscriptions from the Arabic and Egyptian in the deepest part of the third chasm, Poe's most secret message, imply that God ordained the eternal division of black from white in deepest time for all time. It is a fatal omen that Pym does not understand the labyrinth, the walls that are writing and the writings on the wall.

2

P.G	.ÉCIDES	DÉBARRASSE.
LE.	D.SERT.	F.URNIS ENT
AS	HOW.V.R	COR.ESPONDS
.IR.	CAR.E	LONGSEA
F.NE,	HEA.,	.O.SQUE
TE.U	S.ARP	BAR.AIN

—Unintelligible inscriptions on the upper and lower metal plates of Marcel Duchamp's readymade object, *With Hidden Noise*

With Hidden Noise "consists of a ball of twine squeezed between two metal plates secured at the corners by four long screws. The 'hidden' noise refers to an object put inside it by [Walter] Arensberg [Duchamp's patron] who alone knew what it was when he heard it tinkling against the metal."[8]

The ball of twine is both labyrinth and clewline.

Most labyrinths are oriented toward secret knowledge, gnosis, as if breath or word were passed mouth to mouth. Only Arensberg knows until he tells his successor in cabalistic confidence. We may play with our toy, respecting the inscriptions we cannot read, or we may unravel the twine. *With Hidden Noise* is a lesson in the treatment of art and artists. Structuralism may unravel the object,

7 Top view of *With Hidden Noise* (1916). Philadelphia Museum of Art. The Louise and Walter Arensberg Collection.

psychoanalysis may unravel the subject, but to what end? For a tinkling thing the artist did not intend. "There is no solution," said Duchamp, "because there is no problem."[9] But most folk are incapable of such exquisite hauteur.

Certainly Tom Sawyer is incapable of it. "If you'd lay a mystery and a pie before me and him," says Huck, "you wouldn't have to say take your choice. . . . Because in my nature I have always run to pie, whilst in his nature he has always run to mystery."[10] Tom runs to the mystery of stolen diamonds, though in the dream-logic of wish and fear, it is a mystery he himself projects upon the world. *Tom Sawyer Detective* is about the arrogation of adulthood, the diamond of personality.

> "Say, Huck, if we find a treasure here, what you going to do with your share?"
>
> "Well, I'll have a pie and a glass of soda every day, and I'll go to every circus that comes along. . . . What you going to do with yourn, Tom?"
>
> "I'm going to buy a new drum and a sure-'nough sword, and a red necktie, and a bull-pup, and get married."[11]

Huck wants pie, soda, and circuses. He will never be a solid citizen, *but he frees Jim.* Tom wants a sword, a necktie, and a wife. He will be the solidest citizen of all, this zircon of personality. See Tom run to mystery! He chains Jim in order to free him. It is then Jim ruefully observes, Man is free but everywhere in chains.

"When one writes a novel about grown people," Twain tells us in the "Conclusion" to *The Adventures of Tom Sawyer*, "he knows exactly where to stop—that is, with a marriage; but when he writes of juveniles, he must stop where he best can" (221). Twain stops, of course, before marriage but not before he assures us of Tom's fitness for that estate.

> Tom squeezed his small body behind ["a laced and ruffled" Niagara in the "labyrinth" of the McDougal caves] in order to illuminate it for Becky Thatcher's gratification. He found that it curtained a sort of steep natural stair-way which was enclosed between narrow walls, and at once the ambition to

> be a discoverer seized him. Becky responded to his call, and they made a smoke-mark for future guidance and started upon their quest. They wound this way and that, far down into the secret depths of the cave, made another mark, and branched off in search of novelties to tell the upper world about. (191, 177, 191–92)

They find a spacious cavern—shining, bewitching, glittering, fantastic. The labyrinth of Mother Earth issues into that enchanting other world all initiates must chance. By squeezing himself back into her body, Tom ventures toward that rebirth of personality some seek at the peril of their lives and some, like Huck, do not seek at all.

In the blackness of darkness, Tom threads his way with the aid of a kite string—he is the Theseus of our tale, shrewd and nervy: "no commonplace boy," says Judge Thatcher whose daughter plays *femme inspiratrice* (217). The Minotaur, of course, is the murderer Injun Joe, the only other person to discover the secret stairway behind the waterfall. He too chances the labyrinth but he does not have the wit to discover Tom's exit and after Judge Thatcher seals it—sealing too the Age of Heroes—Injun Joe starves to death within. Tom again discovers stolen treasure, $12,000 worth of puberty. He will become a great lawyer, prophesies the Judge, or a great soldier, or both. In the meantime, he gives up piracy for robbery which is more "high-toned" (220), more adult. He dreams of "orgies" (221)—whatever they are—with kidnapped and complaisant women. Injun Joe dreams of tying Widow Douglas to a bed and mutilating her. The American Minotaur is Theseus in feathers, for whom the Widow (Douglas) and the (McDougal) labyrinth are the same.

"Theseus' venture through the labyrinth and the killing of the Minotaur can be construed as a reversal of the birth journey—the hero returning to the woman, encountering a phallic paternal object therein, and destroying it."[12] Theseus' displaced desires are parricidal and incestuous and are achieved only through the assistance of Ariadne who provides the vital twine, the surrogate umbilicus, by which Theseus guides himself back into the mother.

The twine provides him entrance and exit, but it does not guarantee him victory against the Minotaur. He must be courageous as well as opportunistic to undo the power of the parent.

A genial graffito from Pompeii betrays the common appeal of this tale.

8

"The labyrinth," it reads. "The Minotaur lives here." But of course the Minotaur does not live here, and if I take this joke seriously, it is to make a serious point: when the Minotaur escapes the labyrinth, the labyrinth is debased into a mere amusement. In the vulgate of American advertising, Injun Joe is domesticated into ten little Indian hot dogs and the labyrinth debased into an instrument for gluttony.

9

"Get the Rath Wiener to the bun"—and you don't need a ball of twine either. Neither courage nor wit. The kids are the wieners, seduced by Mom. Mom is the bun. Mom is an anatomy of desire, "a-mazed," in our Family Romance.

The Minotaur, in other words, is among us still. In 1960, a naturalist with wonderful eyes, Sr. Picasso, remarked: "If all the ways I have been along were marked on a map and joined up with a line, it might represent a minotaur."[13] Picasso's mask identifies a child at play. Borges's mask, in *Dreamtigers*, identifies an Old Wise Man. "A man sets himself the task of portraying the world. Through the years he peoples a space with images of provinces, kingdoms, mountains, bays, ships, islands, fishes, rooms, instruments, stars, horses, and people. Shortly before his death, he discovers that that patient labyrinth of lines traces the image of his face."[14] Picasso is the greatest maker of minotaurs in our time and Borges the greatest maker of labyrinths. One man's minotaur is another man's labyrinth. Perhaps the Minotaur has taken refuge in Argentina.

The painted caves of prehistory, which date from 30,000–20,000 B.C., were not rediscovered until certain modern explorers, like Lyell and Melville, acquainted us with deep time and not until a child crying "Papa, mira toros pintados!" led her father to a ceiling at Altamira.[15] This genetic tale of wonder is recorded in the year 1879, and though the caves were not authenticated as ancient to the satisfaction of most archeologists until about 1900, they had already been invented to the satisfaction of at least one poet in 1838, in *The Narrative of Arthur Gordon Pym*. Twain's imagination carried him into classical antiquity; Poe's intuition—the intuition of a physicist predicting the existence of a subatomic particle—carried him below time, into a space not yet defined as paleolithic.

At Font-de-Gaume, Les Combarelles, and Niaux prehistoric people discovered the secret of the winding cave—that it is a labyrinthine threshold between profane and sacred zones, even as it is for Twain and Poe.[16]

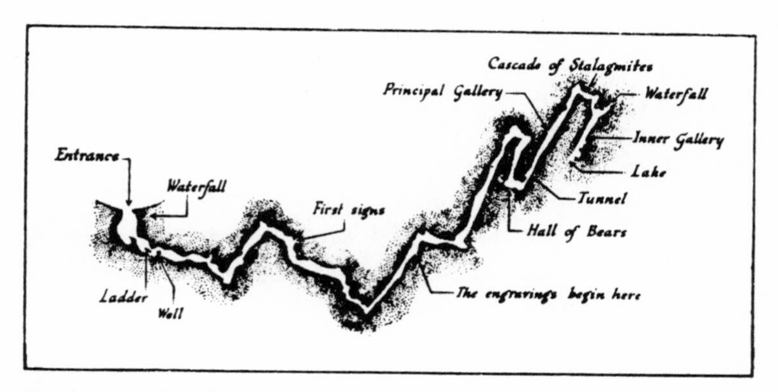

10 An example of fearful passage

In the secret recesses of the cave, where Tom finds the treasure of his manhood and Pym, the word of God, they painted the sacred totems of their tribe. "Reciprocity was [their] aim, a participation in the splendour of the beasts which was of the nature of religion itself, and so required this elaborate separation from normal activities. . . ."[17] The animal art of prehistory is our first evidence of human unconcludedness, and the dangerous winding cave our first metaphor of the soul's uncertain journey, its first rite de passage.

On the island of Malekula, in the Melanesian archipelago, a dead man cannot gain his final resting place until his ghost successfully performs "the ritual of the labyrinth."[18] The ghost must restore half a symmetrical figure erased by Temes Savsap, female guardian spirit of the land of the dead.

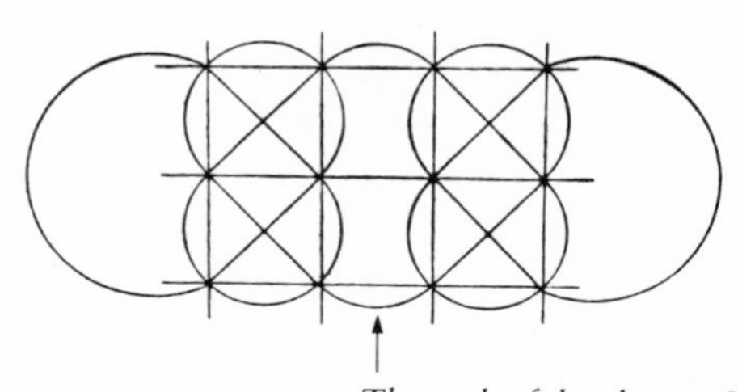

11 The Path *The path of the ghost to Wies*

If he restores it, he passes between the halves to a safe haven. If he does not, Temes Savsap eats him for his witlessness.

The figure originally represented a labyrinth that the initiate was required to trace with one continuous line. As in the child's game, where death and afterlife are not at stake, he was required to trace the figure without lifting his instrument and without repeating himself. The modern Malekulan, however, has "lost the knowledge that the continuous line . . . represents the path" and has come to believe that the path is "the comparatively empty central space" itself (140–41). I do not know if the modern Malekulan ghost squeezes his body, as Tom Sawyer does, through this space; I do know that if he cannot find the track, like Injun Joe he will not survive the trial. Pym, failing to solve the labyrinth, sails straight into the heart of whiteness, a great shrouded human figure who rears herself in a chasm of water. The Terrible Mother starves you to death or eats you alive.

It is possible, incidentally, to draw "The Path" with one continuous line, and the reader is invited to test her wits.

3

12 The pavement labyrinth at Chartres Cathedral

Tesselated into the pavement of many cathedrals during the early Middle Ages, the labyrinth was regarded

> as a symbol of the perplexities and intricacies which beset the Christian's path [or of the] entangling nature of sin or

> of any deviation from the rectilinear path of Christian duty. . . . And it is quite possible that, at a time when the soul had passed out of the crusades and the Church's authority was on the ebb, a journey on the knees around the labyrinth's sinuosities was prescribed as an alternative to these pilgrimages.[19]

In France such a labyrinth was called a *Chemin de Jérusalem* and the goal at the center "ciel" (Heaven) or "Jérusalem" (the holy city). These *chemins* are "unicursal": that is, there is just one path to the goal and there are no false turnings. Perhaps they are models of the Catholic universe: if you work hard and believe truly, you cannot fail to be saved. But since they are not very long—the one at Chartres is only 150 yards—they were perhaps more suitable for children (in their first or second childhoods) than for adults: as devices for penitential play or moral encouragement. You could leave your body in France and travel to the Holy Land in your imagination. And you need not fear that what happens to Spenser's Red Cross Knight will happen to you: that the labyrinth you tread is "multicursal"—full of false turnings—and, beguiled by delight, you end in Errours Den.[20]

In the early Middle Ages, Italian painters began experimenting with perspectival space and the Virgin of the Annunciation received a (holy) book as an attribute. The painter furnishes an imagined depth with figures and furniture; the Virgin, reading or having read, migrates to the enchanting world of Isaiah's prophecy until Gabriel recalls her to her soul self. "Other works of art allow us to keep our consciousness more or less intact. . . . Only the novelist smashes—temporarily—the vessel."[21] A novel like *Tom Jones* is a labyrinth of the world writ large. Like Tom Sawyer in the cave, we are lured from turning to turning, in search of novelties. In honor of Ariadne, Fielding strings us along. Mythological heroes commit themselves to wildly disjunctive experience but return from the other world with elixirs and restoratives. Novel readers commit themselves to mildly disjunctive experience and return from that other and novel world with the spell of its knowledge and power still upon them—even as the Virgin returns with the spell of the biggest novelty of all still upon her, "A Virgin shall conceive."

A riddle is a labyrinth of the world writ small. "In its mythological or ritual context it is nearly always what [is called a] 'capital riddle,'" which you either solve and perhaps win the hand of a princess or fail to solve and forfeit your head.[22] Pericles accepts these conditions and does not fail, but Pericles of course is a prince. The rest of us are doubtless less well equipped. Who, for example, will bet his head on this riddle from the Anglo-Saxon *Exeter Book*?

> Swings by his thigh a thing most magical!
> Below the belt, beneath the folds
> of his clothes it hangs, a hole in its front end,
> stiff-set & stout, but swivels about.
>
> Levelling the head of this hanging instrument,
> its wielder hoists his hem above the knee:
> it is his will to fill a well-known hole
> that it fills fully when at full length.[23]

This riddle seems so straightforward that, like Spenser's Red Cross, you doubtless succumbed at the first false turning. From the disciplined path of the via Christiana you were doubtless tempted into "the wandring wood." The correct answer is a key.

There is another kind of riddle, however, not seemingly straightforward, which plunges us into a confusion so immediate that no turning is more tempting than any other. "What walks on four legs in the morning, two legs in the afternoon, and three legs in the evening?" Like Temes Savsap, the Sphinx eats anyone who fails to answer correctly, and she eats everyone until Oedipus answers "Man"—because a baby crawls on all fours, an adult stands on his own two feet, and an ancient of days needs a cane. Oedipus becomes the embodiment of his insight—a man—and the Sphinx throws herself off a cliff in signal of his mastery.

As the key riddle and *Tom Jones* are homologues of temporal continuity, the Oedipus riddle and *The Sound and the Fury* are homologues of spatial simultaneity. Four legs in the morning, two legs in the afternoon, three legs in the evening: it is like an idiot talking. We come out the other end of *Tom Jones*; we do not come out the other end of *The Sound and the Fury* because there is no other end to come out of. Our goal, so to speak, is not beyond the labyrinth but within it. The four parts of the Compson saga, each part superimposed upon the one before, surround us and gradually clarify one another as Faulkner's narrators become more lucid: the idiot of the first part is succeeded by a brilliant madman in the second, a short-sighted partisan in the third, and an objective observer in the last. The contours of the saga we first failed to grasp become intelligible even as we solve the riddle of the Sphinx (if we do solve it) on normalizing the apparent idiocy of the clues.

Faulkner's novels are "delays in language" even as Duchamp described his painting on glass, *The Bride Stripped Bare by Her Bachelors, Even*, as a "delay in glass."[24] The "labyrinth of . . . consciousness," as James called it, becomes the labyrinth of language itself.[25] All labyrinths embody the principle of delay. Joyce suggested 300 years for the penetration of *Finnegans Wake*.

Ecclesiasticus "declares that the aspirant walks in 'crooked ways' wherein he is tormented by the laws and discipline of Wisdom before he finally wins her by the 'straight way.'"[26] Having walked in crooked ways, Tom Jones gains Wisdom—Sophia—as Christian walks the spiralform of sin and gains the Celestial City. As Father Brown is an unsuspecting aspirant to sainthood, the detective of hardboiled fiction is an unwilling aspirant to herohood. Oedipus charges himself with unpolluting Thebes; the detective of Dashiell Hammett's *Red Harvest* is hired to "clean up" Personville (sometimes and ominously pronounced Poisonville), South Dakota.[27] He just *dreams* of parricide and incest. He claims that catching murderers is just a job and heroism just a "poetic" convention, but we know better: cleverer and more courageous than the rest of us, he straightens a crooked way.

The clues of a detective and the clewline of Theseus are cognate, for a *clue* (previously spelled *clew*) also means "a ball of yarn or thread" (OED). Without a clewline a detective cannot straighten the way along which he finds the clues. If he loses his clewline, he loses himself in a multicursal labyrinth without knowing, as we say, which way to turn. Indeed, if he loses the clewline, he loses the way and the life. In the modern Italian novel *Il Contesto* by Leonardo Sciascia (*Equal Danger* in America), Detective Rogas is unexpectedly murdered at the penultimate moment, and the case on which he is working remains unsolved and unclosed. Sciascia deprives us of that closure that ordinarily makes the detective story such a fine restorative. "If we can make the puzzle work out, we emerge with our sense of mastery over the world reaffirmed."[28] But if we fail to make the puzzle work out—if we fail to unconnect the bent nails—we are newly frustrated. Or worse. Dupin's own opinion is that if he had not succeeded, he might well have been murdered. (Sherlock Holmes, in fact, *is* murdered—then, in a manner of speaking, is reborn.) "The Purloined Letter" is a comedy of manners.[29] Fellini's protagonist in the *Satyricon* is confronted by the Minotaur but wheedles his way free. I'm just a student, he says. He might have said, just a reader of novels.

4 A tenth-century inscription in the Church of San Savino at Piacenza reminds us that the labyrinth represents the world we live in, broad at the entrance but narrow at the exit, so that one who is ensnared by the joys of the world and weighted down by vice can regain the doctrine of life only with difficulty.[30] This text is an allegory of anal rebirth. So Tom Sawyer wanders through the bowels of Mother Earth, then "pushes his head and shoulders through a small hole" (201), and escapes the McDougal caves. So we come out the other end of *Tom Jones*. The intestines of the stomach and the convolutions of the brain are the two primary human labyrinths. Tom's journey is an allegory of alimentation through the intestines; his escape from the body of the mother implies birth into a new state of being. The Virgin's journey is an allegory of mentation through the convolutions: her escape from the body implies the parthenogenetic birth of the second and unselfconscious self that migrates into the world of her text.

The goal of every labyrinth is either within or beyond. The spatial distinction between outside and inside, the special character of inner space, encourages the visual artist to construct a labyrinth whose goal is within. As, let us say, at Chartres or Hampton Court. The temporal distinction between beginning and ending, the presentational aspect of literature, encourages the writer to construct a labyrinth whose goal is beyond. For instance, the first word of Robbe-Grillet's novel *In the Labyrinth* is "I," the last is "me," and nowhere else does the ostensible narrator appear as subject or object. "I am alone here now, under cover" expresses his incarceration in subjectivity. The novel then recounts a soldier's mission and death before the narrator issues from the labyrinth of city, story, and subjective case: "the series of long hallways, the spiral staircase, the door to the building with its stone step, and the whole city behind me."[31]

Like the cave and the castle (Marabar and Marienbad), the city as labyrinth is a recurring *topos*. Daedalus constructs Joyce's Dublin. The Minotaur flourishes in Camus's Oran.[32] K., a land-surveyor, attempts the labyrinth of his village. "The street he was in . . . made toward [Castle Hill] and then, as if deliberately, turned aside. . . . At every turn K. expected the road to double back to the Castle"[33] but it never does and never will and K.'s silly assistants are as useless to him as Vergil and Beatrice are useful to Dante in negotiating the spiralform of Purgatory.

Lost in the Garden of Live Flowers, Alice, like K., strives futilely —"wandering up and down, and trying turn after turn"—until she is rescued.[34] Alice becomes a pawn and triumphs as a queen, whereas Barth's Ambrose M——, lost in the fun house of fiction, is doomed as an artist to "construct funhouses for others and be their secret operator";[35] and Yu Tsun, lost in the Garden of Forking Paths, the labyrinth of time, is doomed as a spy to death by hanging.

Borges is responsible for the most complex labyrinth in modern literature, the Universe as the interminable Library of Babel, and the least complex labyrinth, the simple straight line of Zeno's Paradox along which "so many philosophers have lost themselves" and at least one detective loses his life.[36] In "Death and the

Compass" Detective Lönnrot follows the clues and walks into the arms of his murderer, an experience that suggests there is real virtue in not attempting certain labyrinths. "With the charts of all four oceans before him, Ahab was threading a maze of currents and eddies, with a view . . . ,"[37] etc., etc. Ishmael does not attempt the "Cretan labyrinth" (52) of Queequeg's body—he goes to sea as much for pleasure as physic—nor does he attempt the maze of the living whale, though once, string in hand, he wanders through trellised bones in the Bower of the Arsacides.

With a little practice you can solve the Malekulan figure, but, like James's naif, you will search in vain for the figure in the carpet. A work of art is a game to play; M. Dupin is a player. James's naif is a professional critic. Tom Sawyer is a professional child who wants a necktie and a wife and who, like Ahab, has already outgrown the "low enjoying power." Huck, who takes the simplest pleasure in soda and pie, will never outgrow it: there are, after all, certain labyrinths without goals. In the one in the Cathedral at Poitiers you might be a squirrel in a tree, your only reward the pleasure of your play.

13 Notice the feedback loop

Unfortunately, K. is not to Klamm as Dupin is to D——. K. does not play.

Charles Olson

Obeying the Figures of the Present Dance

C*ALL Me Ishmael* (1947) is a book in name only.[1] It is print rendered aural and haptic, a metaphor for manuscript and collage. That is why its sound and shape are so startling. As Olson says of *Billy Budd*: "It all finally has to do with the throat, SPEECH." And therefore, with the breath.

In "Projective Verse" (1950), Olson argued that the projective poet starts "down through the workings of his own throat to that place where breath . . . has its beginnings," where language possesses bodily resonance, "drama has to come from," and "all act springs" (HU, 61); conversely, the nonprojective poet is "print bred" and, insofar as he stays "where the ear and the mind are," is print-bound. Olson, who charts the history of verse as McLuhan the history of media, contends that Anglo-American poetry, with few exceptions, is nonprojective from the post-Elizabethans to Ezra Pound, the methodology of whose *Cantos* "points a way" toward the redramatization of language (HU, 51, 61). *Call Me Ishmael*, a consummate instance of aurality and hapticity in modern literature, is a redramatization of language. For although it is (often brilliant) scholarship and criticism, it is also something much more ambitious, an extrapolation of *Moby-Dick* as a species of projective verse.

"I still have this enormous conviction," Olson told Ann Charters in July 1968, "that I knew what went on inside that cat.

I haven't had that feeling for anyone else, not even my own father."[2] Henry James may have possessed Hawthorne but Olson was possessed by Melville as, in fact, Melville was possessed by Shakespeare. Yet Shakespeare's possession of Melville was not absolute because Melville saw (or claimed to see) the incompleteness of his master: "And if I magnify Shakespeare, it is not so much for what he did do as for what he did not do, or refrained from doing."[3] Melville's possession of Olson was not complete for the same reason and was expressed in similar words: "I had the feeling for what he [Melville] did do and didn't do. And that's important—what he *didn't do*" (OM, 64). *Moby-Dick* is Olson's point of departure, Melville his accomplice, and *Call Me Ishmael* his prophecy of what Melville might have written a hundred years later.

Breath is to act as manuscript is to collage, and Olson advised Cid Corman, the editor of *Origin*, in May 1951,

> to push
> what you have already started (as to the devices of
> presentation) even further—that is, the one man,
> the book, the juxtaposition of varying materials, or
> varying devices, thicken, thicken, PACK, in order to
> set aside any lingering results of "literary" or
> "aesthetics" or "professional" orderings. . . .
>
> [LO, 76][4]

Olson set the typography for *Call Me Ishmael* himself (OM, 11) according to the above prescription and, for the purpose of thickening and packing his text, juxtaposed many ingenious "devices of presentation." For example, the last lines of "What lies under" are printed like this:

> Quote. The American whaling era—in contrast to the
> Basque, French, Dutch and English—
> developed independently
> concentrated on different species of whale
> covered all seas including the Arctic

> yielded on a larger scale than in any other country or group of countries before.
>
> Unquote.
>
> [CMI, 25]

As McLuhan has made abundantly clear, book technology—and this is particularly true in the production of critical and scholarly books—has arrogated to itself the values visuality fosters—what, after several centuries, we have come to experience as the conventions of lineality, sequentiality, and regularity. By merely subverting a typographical convention, Olson rescues into earshot two nouns from an ossified sign language ("..."), breathes speech-force into the quoted passage by metaphrasing it, and he evidently understood that, as he distorted the naturalism of the book, his text would more nearly resemble a manuscript (a page to be read aloud, product of an aural culture) and a collage (a thickened object, product of a haptic one). Between the medieval manuscript which educes speech and the modern collage which educes touch falls the book which educes neither. A book holds its readers at arm's length, but *Call Me Ishmael* demands their unexpected participation.

Olson characterizes Melville as a "scald" (though he himself is the poet of Scandinavian origin and oral delivery), and, *Moby-Dick* aside, he is not in fact concerned with novels but with manuscripts, some of which he publishes for the first time, most of which lead us not to Melville's literary manner but to his private voice. For example, Olson prints a scrap that Melville had entitled: "What became of the ship's company of the whaleship 'Acushnet,' according to Hubbard who came home in her (more than a four years' voyage) and who visited me at Pittsfield in 1850" (CMI, 22). We remember with embarrassment that sentimental yearning for shipmates dead and gone in Melville's late poetry, and we appreciate how unsentimental his remembrance of them here is, how authentic his voice, that we hear it undisguised. It is one way—Olson has many ways—of forcing language into our ears and out of our throats, of forcing us to respond at that physiological place where breath has its beginning.

He will use arcane words like *usufruct*, variant spellings like *hurrikans*, and abbreviations like *N.G.*, all of which look so odd on the page that one is impelled to sound them on the tongue. And there are other such "devices of presentation" as well. More important, Olson, like Whitman, is fond of slang, because it has not yet shed the impress of speech: "You can approach BIG America and spread yourself like a pancake, sing her stretch as Whitman did, be puffed up as we are over PRODUCTION" (CMI, 69). In like manner, Olson willingly distorts the naturalism of the written sentence (a complete thought rendered) and the paragraph (the topic sentence developed). His model for such distortion was D. H. Lawrence's *Studies in Classic American Literature*, and his theoretical justification, Pound's edition of Fenollosa's "The Chinese Written Character as a Medium for Poetry," an essay that silently undergirds "Projective Verse." Olson systematically rescues *Call Me Ishmael* from abstractions of the eye.

Most important of all, Olson does not merely describe his vision of Melville's language; he enacts it. Action Criticism like Action Painting, criticism as enactment. "The cadences and acclivities of Melville's prose change," he writes. "The long ease and sea swell of Ishmael's narrative prose contrasts this short, rent language of Ahab" (CMI, 68). This observation is true, but Olson deliberately exaggerates Melville's contrast between protagonists. The "parts" of *Call Me Ishmael* are shards of language and rapid-fire discourse in Olson's version of Ahab's cadence—staccato, metaphoric, apocalyptic, nervous lofty. The three intercalated FACTS in slow and countermotion are exquisite elongations in his version of Ishmael's. "FACT 2," for instance, is in a plain style so gentle that, though it is composed of a single sentence of 175 words, nowhere in the lull of its ease and swell is that remarkable fact declared. (Similarly, the "LAST FACT" is an uninterrupted sentence of 116 words.) These intercalations—whose genesis is surely the intercalated cetology of *Moby-Dick*—are so conspicuous that even the least perceptive will not only hear but, as of the cetological passages, will experience their greater specific gravity, the sense of the fault lines they create, opening spaces. The distinction between "part" and "FACT," in other words, moves us not merely in a verbal but also in a physiological way, as Robert Duncan understands the way in which *The Maximus Poems* moves him.[5]

"FACT 2,"—"the longest sentence Olson ever wrote"—is called "dromenon." Ann Charters quotes Olson who quotes Jane Harrison's *Ancient Art and Ritual*:

> "The Greek word for a *rite* as already noted is *dromenon*, 'a thing done'—and the word is full of instruction. The Greeks had realized that to perform a rite you must *do* something, that is, you must not only feel something but express it in action, or, to put it psychologically, you must not only receive an impulse, you must react to it. The word for rite, *dromenon*, 'thing done,' arose, of course, not from any psychological analysis, but from the simple fact that rites among the primitive Greeks were *things done*, mimetic dances and the like." [OM, 56]

I am suggesting that, as nearly as literature can, *Call Me Ishmael* is the performing of a rite, a dance, and it shares with much Abstract Expressionist painting and sculpture the character of a gnosis that, as the critical reception of *Call Me Ishmael* indicates, attracts those who are privy to its uses and repels those who are not. The dust wrapper for the original edition claims that it is "that rare and perfect thing—a work of scholarship that is full both stylistically and conceptually of the greatest excitement and movement" (OM, viii) and although one suspects that Olson, again like Whitman, had a supervisory hand in his press notices, one nevertheless agrees with this judgment. Evidently heeding the notion he would later formulate in "Projective Verse," that "ONE PERCEPTION MUST IMMEDIATELY AND DIRECTLY LEAD TO A FURTHER PERCEPTION" (HU, 52), Olson did this thing at great speed in less than four months.

Olson finished the 400-page first draft of *Call Me Ishmael* in 1940, but his mentor, Edward Dahlberg, found the "Hebraic, Biblical Old Testament" style inappropriate, and Olson never revised his manuscript. He wrote the much shortened version we now have "at a clip" between April 13, 1945, and the first week of August 1945 (OM, 9). He was thirty-four years old. Like Jackson Pollock, who began his Drip Paintings in 1947 at the age of thirty-three, Olson came relatively late to his artistic maturity, and perhaps for the same reason. The early work of the Action Painters is often a disguised representation of mythical subject matter, but as these artists mature they learn a radically new technique for the presentation of myth: a technique of freely associating, a controlled undercutting of consciousness in the act of creating. Olson describes it in "Projective Verse" as the "process" of poem making: "get on with it, keep moving, keep in, speed, the nerves, their speed, the perceptions, theirs, the acts, the split second acts, the whole business, keep it moving as fast as you can, citizen" (HU, 53). De Kooning, it used to be said jokingly, could paint at ninety-eight miles per hour, and that is no time for a novice to make split-second decisions. At most, a plasmatic figuration remains in Pollock's high-speed Drip Paintings, and what becomes highly visible is not the representation of myth but the enactment of process, not a myth of creation but the uncreated Word itself. Pollock and Olson create sacred works in the mythological present, "the context of / Now!" (M, 22).

Olson invariably uses blank and nearly blank pages whenever he shifts from part to FACT and vice versa as a way of sharpening the fault line between them. He always places the title of each part or FACT in thickened capitals and approximately a fourth of the way down from the top of the page and always begins his text approximately a third of the way up from the bottom; at least in part for the sake of breath. Again we are reminded of his advice to Cid Corman:

> give the 1st piece in any issue
> an open page ahead of itself: not necessarily a whole
> white page, in fact, on the contrary, i think not: but
> give it some breath, the reader, to, start anew with,
> the material, after, the intros[.]
>
> [LO, 65]

But elsewhere Olson tells Corman that "graphics was, once, a little bit my profession: Ben Shahn and I were, once, a 'team'" at the Office of War Information during the Second World War (LO, 52). The design of each title page—the relation of type and type face to space—suggests the asymmetrical ordering of Bauhaus art, and we may describe the first page of each section in words Olson used to advise Corman about the cover of *Origin*: "a simple straight space, presenting itself in one glance, gains . . . by severity & formality" (LO, 67). In fact, one is constantly discovering interesting indentational patterns, oddly shaped paragraphs, arguments by design and formula that present themselves, like geometric abstractions, in a single glance. A conventional book does not exist in such an aesthetic space—it does not exist in aesthetic space at all—but *Call Me Ishmael*, which does, is not merely a work of conceptual and stylistic but of visual excitement and movement, and perhaps that is why it is also imaginable as a film. Imagine, for instance, the FACTS narrated (as Orson Welles used to introduce his films with a narration) as the events described therein are enacted in grainy gray, in slow motion, and in silence.

As speech is the "solid of verse"—the aural become palpable—*Call Me Ishmael* is a metaphoric collage composed of various intercalated planes small and large: syllables, words, fragments, a prefatory poem, a note of thanks (on the fortieth page), a dedication on the eighty-eighth (again the syntax of the book broken open), blank pages, pages asymmetrically ordered, FACTS, and parts—just as in some not strictly comparable sense *Moby-Dick* is a collation of genres—sermon, poem, dictionary, affadavit, encyclopedia, epic, drama, short story. In Olson and Melville these solids are of varying textures, sizes, weights, intensities, speeds of motion and direction in space, and degrees of transparency and verisimilitude; their interrelations, like the interrelation of objects in projective verse, "are to be seen as creating the tensions of [the work of art] just as totally as do those other objects create what we know as the world" (HU, 56). A conventionally organized book, like a painting by, say, Raphael, means to be, whatever else, the representation of a symbolic structure; *Call Me Ishmael*, like a painting by, say, Pollock, means to be, whatever else, the presentation of a physical object. Olson's unexpected capitalization of important words is a poet's device, a kind of shout, or a painter's, a way of implying the scale of a word's significance by an equivalent physicality.

Though Olson himself slides into the language of modern art criticism with his talk of tension among objects and "planes of expression" and though in *Call Me Ishmael* he incorporates a certain amount of syntactic and typographic distortion, he neither treats Melville as a subject for sheer verbal abstraction (as Gertrude Stein treats Cézanne) nor fractions objects into the sometimes indistinguishable planes of Analytical Cubism. *Call Me Ishmael* always remains literature for use, a verbal and visual object possessing both speech force and significant form. It is not like that modern hybrid of language and design, the painting-poem (vide Frank O'Hara and Jasper Johns) but like that ancient aural-haptic compound, the ideograph (vide Pound). *Call Me Ishmael* means to be a hieroglyph. But what does a hieroglyph mean?

2 If Nature is a book, as Sir Francis Bacon averred, then reading her letters will win her secrets. There will be a conjunction between the two, the reader will be able to "match" them, and book knowledge will be power. Reading the book of Nature, the supreme act of visuality, became and remained the means of controlling her until the nineteenth century discovered that the letters and the secrets were no longer matchable. It is appropriate that I quote Melville on this discovery: "Say what some poets will, Nature is not so much her own ever-sweet interpreter, as the mere supplier of that cunning alphabet, whereby selecting and combining as he pleases, each man reads his own peculiar lesson according to his own peculiar mind and mood."[6] Similarly, painters in the Renaissance inaugurated a full-scale effort to "match" Nature on canvas. But to reduce a three-dimensional reality to a two-dimensional surface is an illusionist act, the conversion of a haptic reality into a visual one, a means of depotentiating Nature. Mimetic art, like reading, is an act of overlordship, a stance taken

toward reality (whatever the local differences) adopted by virtually every important painter from Raphael to Courbet—until the Impressionists realized that "making" not "matching" (invention, as Emerson said, not imitation) was the key to the new art, that a painting was not, in the first instance, an act of mimesis.

Olson introduces this argument into *Call Me Ishmael*: "As an artist Melville chafed at representation. His work up to *Moby-Dick* was a progress toward the concrete and after *Moby-Dick* a breaking away" (CMI, 42–43). The alphabet of Nature, in other words, had become indecipherable hieroglyphs—things in themselves—like those markings on the bodies of Queequeg and the Whale. The matcher Ahab, irritably reaching after fact and reason, tries to decipher the markings and dies crying his blindness; the maker Ishmael, adopting a different stance, squeezes sperm and the hands of his fellow seamen, and lives in the final reciprocity of Nature. Melville's heroes incarnate the two kinds of will (stance or posture) Olson discerned in history.

In the beginning,

> from 3378 BC (date man's 1st city, name and face of creator also known) in unbroken series first at Uruk, then from the seaport Lagash out into colonies in the Indus Valley and, circa 2500, the Nile, until date 1200 BC or thereabouts, civilization had ONE CENTER, Sumer, in all directions, that this one people held such exact and superior force that all peoples around them were sustained by it, nourished, increased, advanced, that a city was a coherence which, for the first time since the ice, gave man the chance to join knowledge to culture and, with this weapon, shape dignities of economics and value sufficient to make daily life itself a dignity and a sufficiency. [HU, 19]

This is the "FIRST WILL" of Neolithic man, whose shadow Olson recognized in Yucatan where he lived from December 1950 to July 1951 and where he daily experienced the descendants of the Maya (themselves, he speculates, descended from the Sumerians) and the ancient Mayan hieroglyphs. The experience of Mexico, the primer and trigger of primitivity, evidently produced as great a "culture shock" in Olson as the descent into Polynesia produced in Melville—though, like the corrupted islanders of *Omoo*, the contemporary Maya are, to a necessary extent, fallen: "They are poor failures of the modern world, incompetent even to arrange that, in the month of June, when the rains have not come far enough forward to fill the wells, they have water to wash in or to drink. They have lost the capacity of their predecessors to do anything in common" (HU, 6).

What the Maya, those extraordinary people who domesticated maize, once possessed in the spirit of the First Will was "the management of external nature so that none of its virtu is lost, in vegetables or in art" (HU, 8). In that unfallen time, according to Olson, that management "kept attention so poised that . . . men were able to stay so interested in the expresson and gesture of all creatures, including at least three planets in addition to the human face, eyes and hands, that they invented a system of written record, now called hieroglyphs, which, on its very face, is verse, the signs were so clearly and densely chosen that, cut in stone, they retain the power of the objects of which they are the images" (HU, 7). As a mode of art the hieroglyph enacts no less than represents the forms of Nature, at once ideographic and phonetic. As a work of art it mediates between "the very formalism of which the maya were masters [i.e., abstraction]" and the risk that "never got out of hand (out of media) as did the architecture & the pots, running, to naturalism" (SW, 110). Olson's notion of the prelapsarian primitive describes an ecological poise of objects and forces (including man as object and force) unobstructed by ego.

In Sumer the Fall is into incoherence: "just about 1200 BC . . . something broke . . . a bowl went smash" (HU, 19). So, too, in Mexico: "When the attentions change / the jungle leaps in / even the stones are split" (SW, 169: "The Kingfishers"). So, too, in Greece, the attentions change: "Homer was an end of the myth world from which the Mediterranean began" (CMI, 117). Odysseus is complected of the Second Will, the will to "*search, the individual responsible* to himself," which in its ultimate egocentrism is Ahab's madness (CMI, 118). But if "the true self is not an asserting function but an obeying one" (SVH, 45), then where is the man of right action who obeys dictates deeper than appetite and obsession, the man of obedience?

"He who possesses rhythm possesses the universe" (HU, 10), claims Olson, even as Ishmael obeys the alternating rhythm of his blood, assertive Ahab and passive Queequeg, world without end. Ishmael practices an ecology of spirit and possesses a methodology of management toward the Whale and himself. He is the higher third of the hieroglyph, larger than the Ahab and Queequeg he embodies, a foreordination for Olson that "now only, once again, and only a second time, is the FIRST WILL back in business" (HU, 21). At the still point of the Whale Armada, at the World Navel, amid images of gestation and rebirth, Ishmael discovers his own untornadoed center. *Homo maximus* of *Moby-Dick*, Ishmael possesses the universe.

Ahab stands before the Whale and reads his own peculiar lesson. The activity of the Second Will, interpretive and imperialist, "disengages him from the familiar" and removes him from the particular (SVH, 39). But since the particular "is the absolute, because it is in fact the way absolute energy asserts itself," that removal distances him from his universe and estranges him from himself (SVH, 27). Olson advised Ed Dorn how to bridge these distances: "*dig one thing or place or man* until you know more abt that man than is possible to any other man"; "you'll have to dig mss" (BOA, 13). Which is, in fact, what Ishmael, bookman and archeologist, does, and is not Queequeg, whom he discovers, a bodily manuscript in hieroglyph? Queequeg, who cannot read the sacred text, respectfully copies it onto his coffin, and Ishmael, who cannot read it either, discovers that coffin his buoy. Unlike the crew of interpreters aboard the *Pequod* who are all (save Pip) trapped in fixities and definites, Ishmael looks upon the doubloon as he looks upon the Whale and the coffin-buoy, those other cunning alphabets, and concedes just this much: "some certain significance lurks in all things."[7] The man of obedience accepts the unintelligibility of the hieroglyph. Ishmael lies in the sea without anxiety, waiting to be rescued. Daniel Orme, Melville's late protagonist, sits at the sea, his pipe fully smoked, waiting to die. Ishmael floats among sharks as if he were Daniel among lions:

neither distanced from the universe nor estranged from himself. Crossed and christly scars upon his chest, Daniel Orme sits at the sea as if he had learned

how to dance
sitting down
[M, 35]

3 In 1929, under the tutelage of Constance Taylor, Olson took lessons in the proto-dance of posture exercise;[8] he tells us about his experience in "Maximus, to Gloucester," Letter 14 (1953) of *The Maximus Poems*, under the heading "on how men do use / their lives":

"to tend to move
as though drawn,"
it also says

Or might it read
"compare
the ripe sun-flower"?

Dance is the art of obedience: to tend to move as though drawn. Dance is the insignia of wholeness: the mandala of the ripe sunflower. Dance is the discovery of posture, of Adam or ape, and if you can "get the posture / to pass from the neck of, / to get it down, / to get the knees bent," then

after the head is clear,
after the burst
a sash-weight does hang
from between the legs
[M, 60–61]

Dance as the stance of process sexualizes the world in perpetual enactment and provides final knowledges in the body—the sense of a sash-weight—knowledges that poetry can never provide. The stance of dance is obedience to First Will, to the restoration of that field of force that includes you, "if you are drawn, / if you do unite." "You might say that I teach posture," Olson replied when asked what he taught at Black Mountain (OM, 84).

Olson knew on his pulses the exhilaration and expressivity of dance:

> I believe, for example, that all men and women can dance—and this alone is enough to establish expression—that all other expression is only up from this base; and that to dance is enough to make a whole day have glory, granting that work is called for of each of us. The hook is that work will always make sense if dancing is understood to be—expression is—the other issue of a day. [LO, 172]

Not just a balletomane (one mad about ballet), Olson struck up a friendship in the mid-thirties with the famous dancer and choreographer Leonid Massine, who evidently obliged Olson by giving him a bit part in the Ballets Russes de Monte Carlo production of *Bacchanale*. Olson's colleague in balletomania, John Finch, recounted the event:

> He was to amble on, taller than a dream giant [Olson was 6 feet 8 inches], and lie down full length on the stage for a time, while tiny ballerinas in Dali costumes swirled and swarmed above him. Then slowly, dreamlike, he was to rise and amble off. All this he did. All this I saw. Where they found tights to fit him, I never learned. And the ballerinas must have been warned about him, for prone and vast, he blocked off most of down-stage left and they detoured around him. But Charlie was very good, calm and poised, a dreaming presence. Motionless, he danced his best dance.[9]

Olson's "Syllabary for a Dancer" (a Black Mountain document though not published until 1971) contains material that he later reworked in "Tyrian Business" (Letter 8 of *The Maximus Poems*). The "Syllabary" is dedicated to an Indian dancer "whose people did not have to lose coherence as much as we of the west did who were led to disperse." Olson asks her to "teach us what you know about sitting," to teach us who "don't even yet know how to sit down, how to dance sitting down!" So Finch's praise is perhaps not beside the point—that "motionless, [Olson] danced his best dance"—and we may compare such praise with Olson's own rude assault on the unnamed Martha Graham in "Tyrian Business," an assault even more rudely cast in the "Syllabary," where she exemplifies those who cannot sit: "such monsters of the old [i.e., the Second] will like a creature such as Martha Graham (who is so far back she craves to be scalped and dragged over the ground and so, because nobody has dragged her, she has everybody do it, she does it, she makes dance an enemy!)"[10]

Olson evidently wanted an intellectual analysis of dance more complete than his "Syllabary" and urged Corman to publish "an investigation into, the whole question of, where dance is, as an *art*, now," and offered him the benefit of several dicta. For example, "any player is (has to be) 1st dancer." Why? Because dance is the "*graphic of drama*" and below it expressively, because the voice and verse of an actor work out of and against motion. With "the body as instrument," Olson recommends an "investigation of dance as [a] problem of space (not, time & not all act)" (LO, 82). Why space? Because dance is the primary artistic means for dissolving unreal boundaries between self and other. Dance is a metaphor for the management of self suspended in the world. Dance returns you to egoless reciprocity, to the condition of Ishmael in the sea at the end of *Moby-Dick*. One who dances lives like a part of the poem of the world. For Olson the dancer's life-become-art is managed as much for use ("to watch / parades, never / to tire") as for beauty, the vernacular aesthetic of New England. The dancer is always space-creating and glyph-enacting, and Olson marvels in a letter to Corman: "You shld see what movements, gestures, investigations of nature these [Mayan] glyphs, contain" (LO, 82). A hieroglyph is a world in dance.

    the art of the language of glyphs
IS
    motion in [space-] time on stone
                                        [LO, 85]

The editor of *Origin* is supposed to choreograph a "dance of mss" with each issue. When he succeeds, he earns Olson's highest praise:

> if you ain't *the god damn best*
> *editor* since when
> (since ever such leading on a dance
> of mss, such a man
> to compose a collective? where, has there been, such
> a man as Cid
> corman—core-
> man (chore-
> agos)?
>
> [LO, 102]

But if Corman is chore-agos, what of Olson who tutored him? And if *Origin*, predicated on Olsonian principles, is a dance, then what of *Call Me Ishmael*, that "thing . . . of the greatest excitement and movement"?

In 1951 Olson wrote the scenario "Apollonius of Tyana"—"A Dance, with Some Words, for Two Actors." Apollonius, a near contemporary of Christ, is a dancer in Olson's version; Tyana, the city, from whose arms he emerges and into whose arms he ultimately returns. Apollonius is bound to her in birth and rebirth: he comes back voluntarily as he is pulled back, as he obeys, because he and Tyana are, in Olson's image, like magnets in a field of force. Their relation is one of health not sickness, and we may trace Melville's unconscious symbols of a similar relation, his transit in health from the mother to the mother, individualism to individuation.[11] Like the *Odyssey*, *Moby-Dick* is an "act of anticipation" that prophesies the psychic development of Western man (CMI, 118). Odysseus breaks through the uroboros of First Will, primal and mediterranean, into the exercise of the Second, the necessary potentiation of consciousness, entry into that outer space Ahab takes as his natural province.

By the nineteenth century, however, Western psychic well-being depended not on the separatist development of ego but on the reintegration of consciousness into the maternal round: Ishmael's destiny is to return at will and in obedience to the mandala of the vortex. From Coleridge, Goethe, and Melville to Joyce, Henry Moore, and Jackson Pollock there has been, in our patriarchal and fiercely technologic time, a powerful reexpression of maternal primitivist imagery, but whether it augurs new birth (is credible evidence that "the FIRST WILL [is] back in business") or whether it merely represents a nostalgic wish fulfillment (a cry for coherence that can never again be answered), I cannot say. Olson's position is a little like Melville's at the end of *Billy Budd*: Billy will triumph in eternity but Claggart is triumphing in time, in the news media. Olson's enthusiasm, in other words, is tempered by the existent culture. "Pejorocracy is here," he says in *The Maximus Poems*, addressing those Melvillean "Isolatos"—"Isolated persons in Gloucester, Massachusetts," in the country Melville once called Anathema (M, 3, 12).

Like Ishmael, like Maximus, Apollonius is a measurer; like Adam, he is configured in a Leonardan mandala. A traveler through all the compass points of the world, he is a missionary for First Will whose quandary is ours: how to redeem a world that has lost coherence, squandered the knowledges of primitive man, debased the identity of objects: "*his* job, at least, is to find out how to inform all people how best they can stick to the instant, which is both temporal and intense, which is both shape and law" (HU, 34). The dance of Apollonius "is a wide investigation into the local, the occasional"; his problem as dancer is "how to extricate what he wants from the mess he is surrounded by, how to manage to locate what he himself feels: that life as spirit is in the thing, in this man" (HU, 35). In these men dancing.

> they dance
> what it is   what it is to say wherein it lies
> where beauty lies
>   that men containeth
>   at this hour
>   [AM, 8]

To dance is to discover "the thrust / of what you are, . . . the hidden constance of which all the rest / is awkward variation"

(AM, 79). The dancer em-bodies his particularity, the nourishment of his beauty. Nor is there dance without love: "no dance / outside the modes and figures of that trance" (AM, 3). Because love is the trance, the ring dance whose leader is Christ. The wisest man, like Apollonius, is the dancer who obeys the dance. So *The Maximus Poems* begin:

> Off-shore, by islands hidden in the blood
> jewels & miracles, I, Maximus
> a metal hot from boiling water, tell you
> what is a lance, who obeys the figures of
> the present dance

Maximus, a baptized and tempered lance like Ahab, is obedient like Ishmael. Obedient to what? To the present dance of syllables. "For from the root out, from all over the place, the syllable comes, the figures of, the dance" (HU, 54). In "Projective Verse," Olson argues the necessity of listening to the syllables forty hours a day, constantly and scrupulously; Maximus is a man of aesthetic action, like that first American Maximus, a carpenter, who undoubtedly also knew that in the making of a thing his instrument was magical and alive. In "the obedience of his ear to the syllables, . . . the dance of the [poet's] intellect is" revealed.

> So, is it not the PLAY of a mind we are after, is not that that shows whether a mind is there at all?
>
> And the threshing floor for the dance? Is it anything but the LINE?
>
> And the line comes . . . from the breath, from the breathing of the man who writes, at the moment that he writes, and thus is, it is here that, the daily work, the WORK, gets in. . . .
>
> [HU, 55, 54 passim]

The syllable is of the ear, in dance; the line is of the breath, in work. Together they perfect a poet's life and the life of Maximus, the Anthropos: "to dance is enough to make a whole day have glory, granting that work is called for of each of us."

Sleeping Beauty Spurned
Remarks on Modern and Postmodern Dance

And David danced before the LORD with all his might; and David was girded with a linen ephod. So David and all the house of Israel brought up the ark of the LORD with shouting and with the sound of the trumpet. And it was so, as the ark of the LORD came into the city of David, that Michal the daughter of Saul looked out at the window, and saw king David leaping and dancing before the LORD; and she despised him in her heart. . . . And Michal the daughter of Saul came out to meet David, and said, How glorious was the king of Israel to-day, who uncovered himself to-day in the eyes of the handmaids of his servants, as one of the vain fellows shamelessly uncovereth himself! And David said unto Michal, It was before the LORD, which chose me above thy father, and all his house, to appoint me prince over the people of the LORD, over Israel: therefore will I play before the LORD. . . . And Michal the daughter of Saul had no child unto the day of her death.—2 Samuel 6

AS the twentieth century dawned, the classical ballet slept—or, in Doris Humphrey's witty remark, "suffered from arrested development—a permanent sixteen, like the Sleeping Beauty herself," isolated from human expressivity.[1] That the dance should puritanize itself is, of course, ironic, for at least since Cicero, who proclaimed that "no sober person dances," it has been a conventional object of scorn for moralists. Increase Mather, for example, whose denunciation is entitled "An Arrow Against Profane and Promiscuous Dancing Drawn out of the Quiver of the Scriptures" or the Puritan Endicott of Hawthorne's

"The Maypole of Merrymount" who orders his colleague to shoot the docile dancing bear through the head because he suspects witchcraft in the beast. What devil incarnate might he have suspected in the Roman elephant who, "corrected by his dancing-master for his unskillfulness, was found practicing his steps by moonlight"?[2]

Sleeping Beauty slept until Michael Fokine, a prince of the royal household, waked her with a kiss. His renovating injunctions, however, were clearly within the tradition of the eighteenth-century reformer Jean Georges Noverre, and the real assault on ballet came from without, from such revolutionary spirits as Loie Fuller and Isadora Duncan for whom the unnaturalness of balletic posture and gesture was simply unacceptable. Duncan sought in dance "the divine expression of the human spirit" and found in her solar plexus "the temporal home of the soul."[3] She was in Paris at the time. (In Carson City, Nevada, Bob Fitzsimmons kayoed her fellow San Franciscan Jim Corbett for the heavyweight championship of the world. The crucial punch was "something revolutionary and new—a 'solar plexus' blow."[4] Certain mystifications are always necessary, or, as the dance critic John Martin once said, Duncan "had, however crudely and in whatever inaccurate and unscientific terminology, discovered the soul to be what less imaginative men have called the autonomic system."[5] As for poor Corbett he let it be understood that "just an ordinary left-hand hook to the stomach" defeated him, nothing at all revolutionary and new.)[6]

French receptivity to Modern Dance is at least as old as Mallarmé's enthusiasm for Fuller, though it was of a classical dancer that he expressed his famous paradox—the ballerina is not a girl dancing. "*She is not a girl*, but rather a metaphor which symbolizes some elemental aspect of earthly form: sword, cup, flower, etc. and . . . *she does not dance* but rather, with miraculous lunges and abbreviations, writing with her body, she *suggests* things which the written word could *express* only in several paragraphs of dialogue or descriptive prose."[7] In swirling draperies magnified by hidden sticks and cunning light, Fuller literalized that metaphor of elemental forms. "Before our very eyes," said

Isadora, "she turned to many colored, shining orchids, to a wavering, flowing sea flower, and at length to a spiral-like lily. . . ."[8]

Fuller and Duncan before and after 1900, Martha Graham and Doris Humphrey from the 1920s, Merce Cunningham from the 1940s, and (let us say) Yvonne Rainer and Twyla Tharp from the 1960s: the tradition of Modern Dance lies in its discontinuity. Martha Graham (perhaps with Fuller in mind) rejected the simulation of natural phenomena: "I did not want to be a tree, a flower, or a wave."[9] Merce Cunningham (certainly with Graham in mind) rejected the intimacy of motion and emotion: "I really didn't like [the idea] that a particular movement meant something specific."[10] Simone Forti (with Cunningham in mind) rejected his speed and fragmentation: "The thing I had to offer was still very close to the holistic and generalized response of infants."[11] Modern Dance tends not to build on prior invention—as classical ballet does—but to reinvent itself, and this reinvention is not necessarily narcissistic or exhibitionistic. "When I have danced, I have tried always to be the Chorus," Duncan claimed. "I have never once danced a solo."[12]

Loie Fuller danced at the Paris Exposition of 1900—Isadora watched her and so did Ruth St. Denis. Henry Adams watched the dynamos, and in a famous essay admitted that "in America neither Venus nor Virgin ever had value as force—at most as sentiment." Adams thought Walt Whitman the one major example of an American artist who had "insisted on the power of sex."[13] Would he have revised his opinion in the presence of Walt's disciple Isadora, who believed herself "a mortal incarnation of Aphrodite";[14] who believed the human body was sacred, the noblest art the nude; and who danced in a filmy chiton without a corset, her feet and legs bare, her hair loose?

Adams did not live long enough to appreciate the historical contour of Modern Dance, or he would have known that in that epicycle of Western art Venus and the Virgin would take a small revenge. Not only are most of the major choreographers in Modern Dance American, most of them are women. Men may have believed or disbelieved Isadora's fantasy of incarnation, but they were *her* fantasies she danced. In a crimson robe she danced the

Marseillaise as if she were Liberty Leading the People. An embattled strain (among the pioneers) expressed a heroic effect. Ellen Terry said she had never seen tragedy until Duncan danced the *Marche Slav*;[15] Ted Shawn chained himself to a rock and danced *Prometheus Bound*; Martha Graham turned *Agamemnon* into a psychodrama called *Clytemnestra*. These are gestures hard to imagine in a Cunningham dancer.

The odd thing about Cunningham's choreography is that it evolved so late: it exemplifies notions of an avant-garde that other arts, like literature and painting, had confronted much earlier. "Dancing," says Cunningham, "has nothing to do with romanticism, sentimentality or love—but with activity";[16] it is an abstraction of the thing itself that excludes narrative plot and psychological characterization, spatial hierarchy and temporal climax. In Cunningham's theater, dancing, music, and décor are independently conceived, then juxtaposed. Each exists in a separate sensory track, and one can no more integrate them than see (or extrapolate from what one does see) all the activity that happens on stage. Cunningham may rearrange the phrases and persons in a dance through chance procedures, reminding us that a definitive version does not exist, and he may collate parts of several dances into a new entity, the so-called Event, which exists for the sake of immediacy in performance but which further tends to unfix our definitions. At his most forbidding Cunningham reinstates an honored function of the avant-garde: *épater le bourgeois*.

The classical dancer conceals stress: though her body be drenched, her smile is fixed. In the choreography of Martha Graham this stress (released backstage in ballet) is shifted onstage as an expressionist attitude: dancers "struggled, wasted themselves, fell, and rose again. Effort was not concealed, it was dramatized. . . ."[17] But in texts that trade in bewilderment or Dada disconcertion, the locus of stress shifts again, from the stage to the audience. In Cunningham's *Winterbranch*, for instance, we peer into darkness made darker still by unpredictable shafts of light; at dancers dressed in black whom we see in bits and pieces, whose actions—sitting, standing, running, walking, crawling—seem painful to them and incoherent to us. We cringe as a powerful stagelight swings toward us, and we suffer noise-music of an excruciating pitch.

Isadora was the first modern choreographer to challenge the remoteness of theater-dancing: she found (she said) "too great a division between the actors and the public" and wished to create for spectators who "would take part more and more in the performance. . . ."[18] The citizen as performer. In *Walkaround Time* Cunningham's dancers idle along the apron of the stage during intermission and chat with members of the audience. The performer as citizen. Some younger choreographers—sometimes called Postmodern—have in fact incorporated untrained citizens in performance, though not necessarily in the spirit of American dancing Duncan would have approved. I am thinking, for instance, of the game-dances of Simone Forti.[19]

Postmodern Dance has sometimes taken to the streets (confuting an older convention of theatrical space) and sometimes measured itself by the clock on the wall (confuting an older convention of theatrical time). It can be fiercely anti-illusionistic, and the purity of Cunningham's exclusion is nothing to Yvonne Rainer's "aesthetics of denial":[20] "NO to spectacle no to virtuosity no to transformation and magic and make-believe no to the glamour and transcendency of the star image no to the heroic no to the anti-heroic no to trash imagery no to involvement of performer or spectator no to style no to camp no to seduction of spectator by the wiles of the performer no to eccentricity no to moving or being moved."[21] What remains is a moving body, and Rainer's NO in thunder condenses an essential impulse of Modern (and Postmodern) Dance, an impulse already implicit in Isadora's rejection of ballet technique: to void dance of all but its ostensible essence, to reveal the real body of the dancer in its "unenhanced physicality."[22]

Nothing of course is harder to reveal, nothing harder to resist than theatrical transformation, and not all Modern (and Postmodern) Dance has meant to resist it. An impulse toward concealment through lighting and costume runs from Loie Fuller to Alwin Nikolais; an impulse toward mythological spectacle, from Ruth St. Denis to Meredith Monk. There is a wonderful moment, a moment full of wonder, in *Sue's Leg* by Twyla Tharp that takes magic and make-believe for a subject of demonstration. A spot-lit performer in soft shoe mimes a tap dance to a Bojangles tape: in three seconds we are as much persuaded that he is tapping as we resist persuasion. Tharp incorporates and alienates us simultaneously; otherwise, we should merely say with Isadora, "Before our very eyes. . . ."

Op Art paintings move (and move differently) before our very eyes in Vasarely, Riley, or the Mondrian of *Broadway Boogie-Woogie*. Kinetic sculpture moves as variously as Len Lye's hula-swaying metal rods or Jean Tinguely's rock-and-rolling machines. Painting and sculpture (I mean) sometimes do aspire to the condition of dance, although the plastic art of the closest structural affinity is film: both "evolve in space and time, and often to music [and] both involve the rhythmical organization of moving images. . . ."[23] It is of course this rhythmical (i.e., choreographed) organization—perhaps the diving sequence in Riefenstahl's *Olympiad* is the most celebrated example—that redeems the medium as an art form. In cine-dance (so-called) the camera becomes an extension of the director's body, its purpose not the photographing of choreography but the choreographing of motion. I am thinking, for example, of Shirley Clarke's exhilarating *Bridges-Go-Round* or the gravely poetic *Pas de Deux* of Norman McLaren.

In the Happening and the dance-theater of Ann Halprin, life itself aspires to the condition of dance; not merely that dance is life in Havelock Ellis's equation, but that life is dance. Creators of the Happening, like Allan Kaprow, insist that the line between the two remain indeterminate, and choreographers like Halprin, whose task-dances may be compared with readymade and found-object sculpture, insist that any motion may be dance (not just "steps," marches, or other stylized deviations from "normal" movement). An event by George Brecht, for example, simply reads:

DIRECTION

Arrange to observe a sign indicating direction of travel.

· travel in the indicated direction
· travel in another direction[24]

Or in the words of the dancer Murray Louis:

> Anyone can dance and most everyone does. Dancing is basically sensing the nature of any motion. If one raised his hand to scratch his head, he would be scratching his head; but if that same person raised the same arm and sensed the weight of those fifteen pounds which comprise that limb, sensed the path through space as the arm rose, sensed that one moment when the finger touched the head, sensed the flexion and extension of the fingers as they scratched . . . then that person would be dancing.[25]

On the other hand, football photos in the *New York Daily News*—"poetry in [*unselfconscious*] motion"—remind us that sport is a kind of dancing just as Merce Cunningham's *How to Pass, Kick, Fall, and Run* reminds us that dancing is a kind of sport. (Knowing how to fall is a necessity, of course, for both dancer and football player.) Many dances, like Balanchine's *Agon*, are, in fact, stylized competitions, though marathon dancing is an endurance contest offensive to both art and play.

The flexible body of Modern Dance, exemplified by Duncan's rejection of the spinal column for the solar plexus, found a natural outpost in McLuhanism. The McLuhanite media priest, Father Culkin, in remarks on educating children, advocated a training in preliteracy: "*Tune up the sensorium.* Go after the kinetic, the tactile, the aural. Rhythm. Structure. Totality. Dance. Dance may be the big thing."[26] This trendy prescription, which fairly implies that dance has moved toward the center of our aesthetic consciousness, dovetails with the testimony of the dancer Carolyn Brown: that dance and TV experience are, or may be, akin—kinetic, tactile, auditory, visceral, essentially nonliterate.[27] But can the experience of television educe a grace beyond the reach of traditional art?

The unframed image on the television screen is not a symbolic spot against the wall, as if it were an easel painting. It is, as it were, the wall itself. Video art easily environs the viewer—I am thinking of an installation at the Whitney Museum in 1982, *Laser Video*, in which Nam June Paik projected moving images of Merce Cunningham onto ceiling and walls. But, as with film, everything depends upon the rhythm of images: "I shut off the sound [of my TV set, says the film-maker Slavko Vorkapich] and try to feel the movements of the screen in my body. It may be a truck passing by, or an old newspaper blown in the wind. And, if these were so organized as to produce in us implicit rhythmic reactions, then we would have filmic choreography."[28] For the education of the young, television will always have teachers of the three R's; it needs choreographers of body consciousness who will organize moving images and inspire young muscles to implicit and explicit rhythmic response. A dance experiment for the health of body and soul. We should not be afraid to encourage the body's response to the sources of rhythm, and we should want to convince those people, like Saul's threatened daughter, who regard that response as a subject of despite. Perhaps an anecdote of the seventeenth century will help.

> It is said that [the indecency of the Fandango] so scandalized the Vatican that its proscription was resolved upon, under pain of excommunication. A consistory having been convoked to try the matter, sentence was about to be pronounced, when a cardinal interfered to say that it was unjust to condemn even the guilty without a hearing: he moved that the Fandango should appear before its judges. This being agreed to as equitable, two Spanish dancers, one of each sex, were summoned. They danced before the august assembly. Their grace and vivacity soon drove the frowns from the brows of the Fathers, whose souls were stirred by lively emotion, and a strange pleasure. One by one their eminences began to beat time with hands and feet, till suddenly their hall became a ball-room; they sprang up, dancing the steps, imitating the gestures of the dancers. After this trial, the Fandango was fully pardoned and restored to honour.[29]

We may draw three lessons from this charming fable: first, that dancing conduces to body consciousness, and "to become conscious of ourselves as body," in the words of Norman O. Brown, "is to become conscious of mankind as one"—even cardinals and

Spanish dancers find it so.[30] Second, as excommunicating dogmas separate people—the operation of Thanatos—so dancing unites them, eroticizing life. And third, dancing vitalizes (redefines) space—hallrooms become ballrooms. The impoverished spaces of Beckett and Max Beckmann are our metaphors of ontological claustrophobia and the figures of Giacometti our metaphors of the manner in which the spaces we inhabit are compressed within the furrows of the flesh. Dance vitalizes the space "of the dancer's real activity, which belongs to him because he himself creates [and] experiences [it] in his own body."[31] In the ancient bull dance at Knossos young men and women grasped the horns of charging bulls—or they failed to grasp them. Though dance no longer issues in blood sacrifice, it is still the art that requires you to put your body on the line, that verifies itself on the pulses. One moral of the story of David and Michal is that for every amateur who risks his dignity dancing, there is another who despises him as a vulgarian. 2 Samuel records life long after the Fall.

Before the Fall or, at any rate,

> at the dawn of civilization, dance had already reached a degree of perfection that no other art or science could match. Societies limited to savage living, primitive sculpture, primitive architecture, and as yet no poetry, quite commonly present the astonished ethnologist with a highly developed tradition of difficult, beautiful dancing. Their music apart from the dance is nothing at all; in the dance it is elaborate. Their worship is dance. They are tribes of dancers.[32]

David the celebrant worships in dance; Michal (ironic and barren) does not. Meredith Monk performed *Juice* with a handful of professionals and eighty-five amateurs, but that doesn't make us a tribe of dancers either. Isadora's prophecy of participation remains unfulfilled. Inside our global village we are neither dancers nor a tribe.

> Primitive men live in a world of demonic Powers. Subhuman or superhuman, gods or spooks or impersonal magic forces, good or bad luck that dwells in things like an electric charge,

> are the most impressive realities of the savage's world. The drive to artistic creation, which seems to be deeply primitive in all human beings, first begets its forms in the image of these all surrounding Powers.[33]

We have naturalized much of the outer world and do not dance to placate gods or spooks: the electric charge that once dwelt in savage now dwells in technologic things. We may environ ourselves in video and we may beget forms appropriate to the power that surrounds us, eductions leading from body consciousness toward bodily grace, the body itself become a tuning fork of sensibility. Or we may not. If Riefenstahl herself choreographed the images, Michal would find ways to resist them, and Michal would be half-right; the movements of the screen we feel in our bodies might well exacerbate a problem it would be folly to ignore—the establishment for some of a privacy too deep for tears.

In his essay "Puppet Theatre" (1810) Heinrich von Kleist mythologized this problem as the ambivalent relation of body consciousness to grace.

> In the organic world we see that grace has greater power and brilliance in proportion as the reasoning powers are dimmer and less active. . . . So, too, when knowledge has likewise passed through infinity, grace will reappear. So that we shall find it at its purest in a body which is entirely devoid of consciousness or which possesses it in an infinite degree; that is, the marionette or the god.[34]

The kinesic of solo dances like the frug suggests marionettes in motion and promises the consolation of the void. Ballroom dancing promises the consolation of consciousness and suggests in its ultimate refinement, the *Liebeslieder Walzer* of Balanchine, a godlike grace. Between the subhuman and the superhuman, the marionette and the god, lies the range of human response. Perhaps we can exploit technology for moral and aesthetic ends and dance in our bones and on our feet.

Perpetual Motions

ONCE upon a time His eye was on the sparrow. He never winked, He never blinked, He never wept, He never slept. His death was reported in due course though some missed the announcement. "Could it be possible? This old saint in the forest has not yet heard anything of this, that *God is dead*!"[1] In any case, James Clerk Maxwell (1831–1879) had already conceived his Demon (1871–1951) who was to keep an undistracted eye on a unit of matter prosier still than the sparrow—the molecule.

Maxwell did not doubt the operation of the second law of thermodynamics in respect to bodies in mass: if the temperature in a vessel of air is uniform, it will remain uniform save through an expenditure of work. His tricky hypothesis concerned the little lower layer: though the mean speed of a great number of molecules is virtually uniform, the speed of individual molecules varies greatly.

So Maxwell divided a vessel into two parts, A and B, leaving a small hole between. The Demon presided at the hole, opening and closing it at will, allowing only swifter-moving molecules to pass from A to B and only slower-moving ones to pass from B to A.

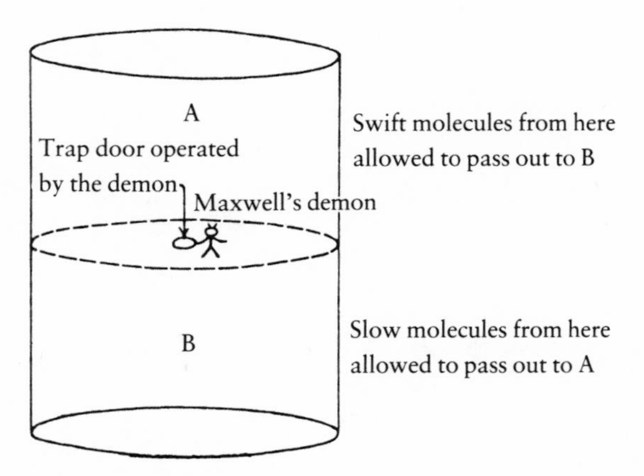

14 Maxwell's Demon poses at the trap door

The temperature of B, Maxwell concluded, would rise in contradiction of the second law: the hotter, expanded air of B would drive a heat engine as long as the Demon sorted. And if the Demon's hardihood were not in question, the engine would run in perpetual motion.

Maxwell also attributed intelligence, free will, extreme smallness, and astonishing eyesight to his Demon, but, like Cassandra Austen on her sister Jane, that hardly tells us anything we wouldn't have supposed and nothing the work itself doesn't imply. The Demon has yet to meet his biographer.

(1) Did the Demon have a sex life? He seems to have been thoroughly mid-Victorian, like that sensitive and celibate fellow in *The Mill on the Floss* who was said to have a hump. *Said* to have a hump because we never really *see* the hump. As the old saying goes: no body, no sex.

(2) Was the Demon happy? This question is a bit more complex, and it would be all too easy to truck out old saws about wage slavery and alienating labor. It is possible, after all, that the Demon was like Stephen Blackpool in *Hard Times*, who worked day and night, like a saint, without complaint. The fact of the matter is that as of now we just don't know whether the Demon was happy or not. My own theory is that he was like the anonymous English-

man of Auden's poem who "satisfied his employers" and "served the Greater Community."

(3) What was the circumstance of his passing? Here we are on firmer ground. Vessels A and B are, optically speaking, a closed black body, and in 1951 Leon Brillouin argued that the Demon could not in fact see the molecules without first introducing a source of light. But the absorption of this light, in part by the Demon, increases the entropy of the system, an increase greater than the decrease the Demon can effect by sorting molecules.[3] To say it differently: the Demon died of old age. His time had come. Toward the end, one of his physicians noted that he "experiences a small recoil every time he lights his torch to emit the speed-probing photon, exactly as a rifleman does when he fires a bullet."[4] Maxwell's Demon could no longer stand the gaff. He could no longer keep his eye on the molecule. His first symptom was a "certain vertigo."

Maxwell did not build a machine for his Demon, but John Nefastis did.

Who is John Nefastis? He is a character in Thomas Pynchon's novel *The Crying of Lot 49* (1966).

Does the Nefastis machine work? If you like. But the Demon will communicate only with a sensitive.

Is Oedipa Maas, the heroine of the novel, a sensitive? She is a woman of religious sensibility.

Are there any sensitives in the novel? There are (to be sure) the deaf-mutes who tango and two-step, waltz and slop, without collision. Oedipa is amazed. Are they responding to "some unthinkable order of music, many rhythms, all keys at once, a choreography in which each couple meshed easy, predestined. Something they all heard with an extra sense atrophied in herself"?[5] It is as remarkable that molecules in a vessel do not collide as it is that a demon sorts them.

Oedipa Maas (OM) is the executrix of Pierce Inverarity's will (PI), and she tries to resolve his endlessly complicated estate. She becomes a sorting Demon and suffers a Demon's fate, the incipience of paranoia. And yet, unless Oedipa goes mad, om will never determine pi. Om is a sacred mantra, pi is an indeterminate number, 3.14159. . . .[6] Oedipa may abolish indeterminacy but she cannot resolve it, even as a geometer cannot resolve the dialectic of square and circle with ruler and compass. That sort of thing happens only in books. "In the beginning," writes Joyce in *Portrait of the Artist*, Stephen "contented himself with circling timidly round the neighbouring square. . . ."

Oedipa's choice, then, is between the beacon of order (i.e., paranoia) and the tropism of disorder (i.e., entropy). Or we may translate Pynchon into Norman Mailer. The tropism of disorder in the body is an entropy of cell growth: cancer. The beacon of order in the body politic is a paranoia of parapolitics: the diffusion of Communist cells, and Big Brother with his eye on every sparrow.

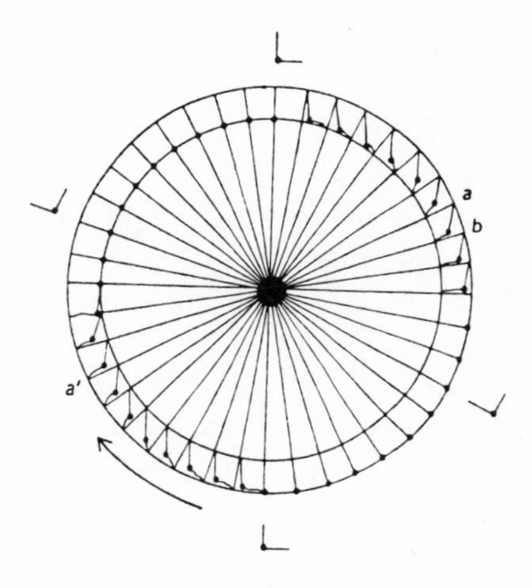

15 The wheel of the Second Marquis of Worcester (1601–1677) had forty spokes and a double rim, the outer fourteen feet in diameter, the inner twelve. Fifty-pound weights flexibly secured between neighboring spokes were meant to overbalance the wheel and establish a perpetual motion. "Be pleased to judge the consequence," wrote the Second Marquis, whom the consequence could not have pleased.

2 In the eighteenth century alcoholics combusted spontaneously.[7] In the nineteenth century masturbators went mad and blind. The pleasure of the imperial self inspires a fantasy of communal resentment. In the twentieth century drug freaks endure "chromosomal damage." There is a nice congruence between the sophistication of science and the sophistication of fantasy.

Overbalancing wheels for achieving perpetual motion are first recorded in medieval Europe and reach their point of greatest complication in the eighteenth century. All of them founder on the first law of thermodynamics,[8] but, if, like Marcel Duchamp, you aspire to a "playful physics," then why not invert a bicycle wheel upon a stool? Suspended and without a tire, the wheel is purified. Spinning in light, a magic circle, it renews the other world. Friction is another name for Time.

16 The bicycle wheel teased Duchamp out of thought. "To see that wheel turning was very soothing, very comforting, a sort of opening of avenues on other things than material life. . . ." (Marcel Duchamp, *Bicycle Wheel*, 1951 [3rd version after lost original, 1913]. Metal wheel [25½″] on painted stool [23¾″]; overall height, 50½. Collection, The Museum of Modern Art, New York. The Sidney and Harriet Janis Collection.)

Sexual intercourse is the model for making fire by friction.[9] There is neither fire nor sexual intercourse in the Garden of Eden. After the Expulsion, however, angels stand guard with a fiery sword. But how can the fiery sword belong to the angels? Obviously it belongs to fallen Adam who "knew Eve his wife; and she conceived and bare 'Cain.'"

Urination is the model for putting fire out. I need hardly recall the example of Gulliver. Urination is the opposite of friction. Urination is play. "Play is [often] an occasion of pure waste."[10]

Awaiting death, Cincinnatus C. leafs through the photographs of a magazine published "once upon a time, in a barely remembered age. . . . Everything was lustrous and shimmering; everything gravitated passionately toward a kind of perfection whose definition was absence of friction." And so it was that life was lost (according to Nabokov) in the divine indiscipline of child's play. "Reveling in all the temptations of the circle, life whirled to a state of such giddiness that the ground fell away. . . ."[11] Reveling in all the temptations of the circle, life and art become discontinuous. Nabokov's dancer squanders the primary illusion of force, the "form-in-the-making"[12] of dance, and becomes mere body.

The idea of perpetual motion is "rooted in the Hindu concept of the cyclical and self-perpetuating nature of all things."[13] Shiva embodies this idea. He is the god whose preeminent activity is dancing. "The perpetual dance is His play."[14] The play of men dancing restores the ancient round. The four seasons in the painting by Poussin dance in a circle to the music of time. "The dance itself has nothing to make it end."[15] The dervish (who whirls and is never giddy) becomes pure spirit.

3 Perpetual motion is a fantasy of feedback, the principle of such self-regulating devices as water clocks and wine dispensers since the third century B.C. The first feedback device of the modern world was the thermostat, invented before 1624 by the Dutchman Cornelis Drebbel, who equipped an alchemical furnace with one in order to maintain the constant temperature he thought necessary for transmuting metals.[16]

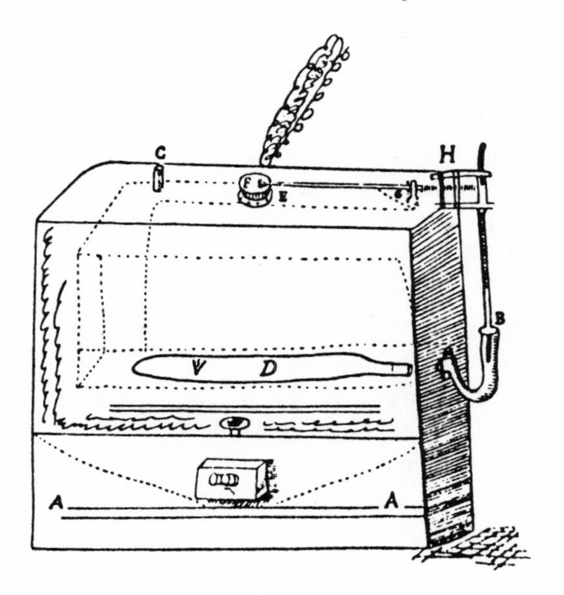

17 Drebbel's thermostat regulates the temperature of an incubator in this drawing by his grandson. Smoke from a fire (A) rises around a water-jacketed incubator (dotted lines) containing a vessel of alcohol (D) sealed by mercury in a U-shaped tube. The smoke escapes at E. When the temperature in the box rises beyond a certain point, the expanded volume of alcoholic vapor pushes the mercury against the rod (B), which, through H, pivots a damper (F) onto E, throttling the fire. When the temperature falls below a certain point, the volume of vapor contracts, the mercury recedes, the rod descends, and the damper opens once again.

The thermostat represents a closed-loop system with negative feedback,

> where a signal travelling once around the loop experiences a change in sign. Since any disturbance [e.g., a change in temperature] automatically causes corrective action in the opposite direction [e.g., an increase or decrease in the supply of heat], a system with negative feedback is self-stabilizing. (A loop without a sign change has *positive* feedback. Instead of tending toward equilibrium, it magnifies the effect of disturbances in spiraling fashion, representing a vicious circle.)[17]

Nabokov's dancer suffers the effect of positive feedback. The Fall is a function of positive feedback.

Ishmael the sailor survives by virtue of negative feedback. Whenever the "hypos" of life on land menace him, he takes to sea as a way of "driving off the spleen, and regulating the circulation." Such corrective action succeeds, and the revolving vortex at the end of *Moby-Dick* is not vicious. It liberates Ishmael into a Peaceable Kingdom: "*The unharming sharks, they glided by as if with padlocks on their mouths; the savage sea-hawks sailed with sheathed beaks.*"[18] Ishmael effects a "temporary and local reversal"[19] of entropy, even as Nature regulates herself on sinking the *Pequod*. Nature flushes herself of soiled human content, and Ishmael floats on the sea like the ball float in a toilet tank.

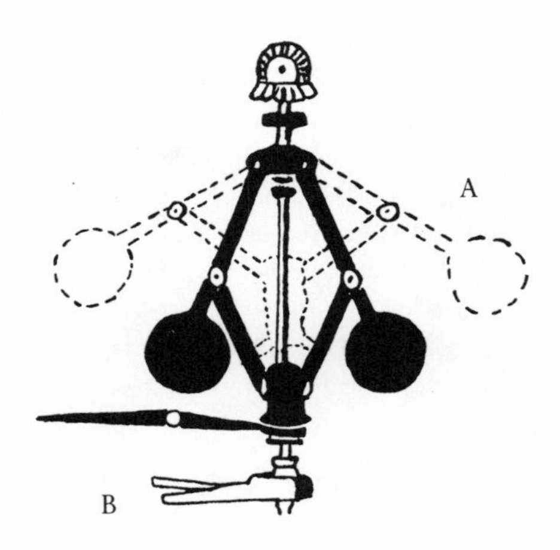

18 James Watt first applied the flyball governor to a steam engine in 1789.

When the balls revolve, raising their levers to position A, they reduce the excess speed of the engine by closing the valve at B. Having reduced the excess speed, the balls lower their levers. In *Sense and Sensibility* Elinor Dashwood regulates her emotions as a governor regulates an engine. When Elinor feels pain, she denies feeling. Having denied feeling, she minimizes pain.

In *Northanger Abbey* Catherine Morland "loved nothing so

well in the world as rolling down the green slope at the back of the house." In *Persuasion* Louisa Musgrove "must be jumped down ['steep flights and stiles'] by Captain Wentworth." In *Sense and Sensibility* Marianne Dashwood runs "with all possible speed down the steep side of a hill."[20] Catherine escapes injury because she is a child. Louisa breaks her crown. Marianne nearly loses her virtue. She falls outside her garden gate, into the arms of her deceiver. Each is tempted by the exhilaration of falling free, though the Fall is never free.

"Heat always runs downhill" is a colloquial paraphrase of the second law of thermodynamics. If any physical system is allowed to distribute its energy its own way, it always does so in a manner that entropy, the measure of energy unavailable for work in that system, increases. Austen's taboo on unregulated pleasure is as irreversible as the second law, although a temporary and local reversal of that taboo—and of entropy too—is available to her in dancing. In *Northanger Abbey* partners at a country dance start down together from the top of a set and finish together at the bottom. Austen, Melville, and Nabokov share the moralism of physical law.

Art consoles us for falling outside the garden, and some art, fecund and luxuriant, reminds us of the Garden itself. *Great Expectations*, for instance. Work may be converted without loss into heat, but heat may not be converted without loss into work. *Great Expectations*, however, seems to contravert the expectations of entropy, as if there were no loss to friction between the mind that imagined and the hand that wrote. Dickens understands the magnitude of this achievement for he lends a playful metaphor of it to Joe Gargery, the village blacksmith. Joe is nearly a saint and nearly without language, but in a burst of eloquence as frictionless as Dickens's own, composes a couplet for his father's tomb. "I made it," says Joe, "my own self. I made it in a moment. It was like striking out a horseshoe complete, in a single blow."[21]

So in *Ulysses* Joyce lends a playful metaphor to Leopold Bloom. Bloom, a virtuoso among schoolchildren, pisses higher than anyone else in his high-school class. And who has written a novel in English that goes higher than *Ulysses*? Dickens and Joyce entrust these metaphors of unexpected accomplishment not to Pip and Stephen but to dearer, older complements, more foolish and more wise.

4 In *Love and Death* Woody Allen dances with Death. Death dissolves in the cordial of comedy, and men grow brazen. "Where is thy sting-a-ling?" asks a character in *The Hostage*, as a dead man rises to an occasion. Comedy restores *la ronde* and the ring of endless light. Comedy confounds death as perpetual motion confounds entropy.

In 1834 Charles Babbage proposed a computer for all arithmetic operations. He intended this machine—the Analytical Engine, as he called it—not only to make sixty calculations a minute but "to modify its course of action according to the outcome of previous calculations."[22] Babbage expressed this notion of feedback as "the engine eating its own tail.[23] A snake biting its tail is a type of uroboric feedback, a closed system in which entropy does not increase. A dragon biting its tail is the principal firework at the fair in *Madame Bovary*. (But it does not ignite. Damp powder.)

Madame De Farge's procedures for storage and retrieval cannot compete with Babbage's punched cards and memory bank. In truth, Madame De Farge is not much at knitting the web of Fate—she is undone, you may recall, by a plucky nanny. Undoing Fate is like dancing with Death. Needless to say, it is the burden of comedy to undo Fate.

"Comedy celebrates the capacity of the human organism to stabilize itself after a shock."[24] I am thinking of that Zen master, about to die, who asked his disciples:

> "I have seen monks die sitting and lying, but have any died standing?"
>
> "Yes, some."
>
> "How about upside down?"
>
> "Never have we seen such a thing!"
>
> Whereupon [the master] stood on his head and died.[25]

The master is master of comedy. He celebrates the capacity of the human organism to stabilize itself after the greatest shock of all.

The function of the governor was (and is) to confer upon the prime mover that greater stability and smoothness necessary for intricate and delicate labor.[26] Watt's work is an analogue of God's. The Great Machine of Nature in eighteenth-century England presupposes a Divine Mechanic, a Governor who governeth all.[27] The Nefastis Machine in twentieth-century America presupposes a Mad Scientist. Elinor Dashwood tends naturally toward the mechanical, Oedipa Maas toward the paranoid. Tess Durbeyfield veers toward the passional: she kills the man who dishonors her. The threshing Machine Tess mounts and serves presupposes the Devil himself—its owner looks like "a creature from Tophet." The thresher is without a governor, and Tess learns its cruel lesson on her body: "her knees [were] trembling so wretchedly with the shaking of the machine that she could scarcely walk."[28] In another time Kafka's harrow pierced its victim's body with Holy Writ. The Word was made flesh in rosy crucifixion. "In the Penal Colony" reminds us that the Old Commandant is now dead and that his machine has gone berserk. Hardy and Kafka record the end of a dispensation.

5 The machines of Rube Goldberg, contraptions of genial disenchantment, never hurt anyone. In 1920 Marcel Duchamp invited Goldberg to contribute a cartoon to *New York Dada*—Duchamp had already discerned the cousinship of Dada and Pop. In fact, *The Bride Stripped Bare by Her Bachelors, Even* (1915–1923) bears a family resemblance to a Goldberg Variation.

The Bachelors never do make love to their Bride, but at least she has a body. Lawrence's Women in Love don't have bodies. Ursula and Gudrun refute the old saying which I thought was irrefutable: no body, no sex. Ursula "was reminded of the Invisible Man, who was a piece of darkness made visible only by his clothes."[29] Ursula and Gudrun wear clothes, which makes them visible. Otherwise

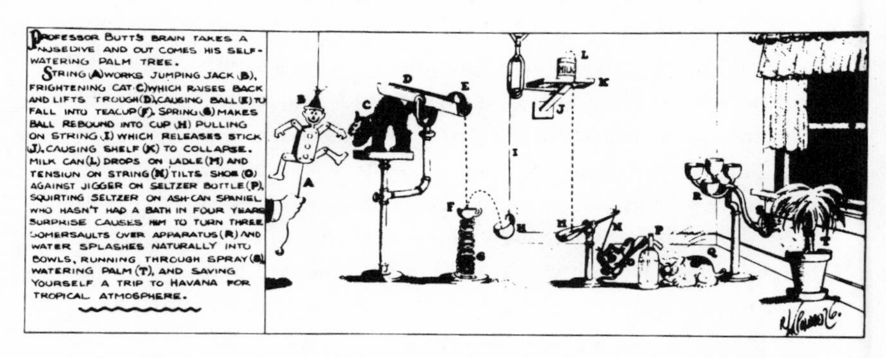

19 *Professor Butts's Brain Takes a Nosedive (Self-Watering Palm Tree)* (Rube Goldberg, c. 1930). When Professor Butts pulls the string on his jumping jack, he converts motive force into the prolongation of desire. From string-phallus to self-watering palm, hand to hand in masturbatory realization. Copyright © King Features

they too would be invisible. Their clothes are stylish because Lawrence is an excellent couturier.

When the Invisible Man takes off his clothes, he threatens us. By exposing himself, he reminds us that the self is a fiction. Maxwell's Demon does not threaten us: he is modest and tame, like the ghost in Babbage's machine. "The Analytical Engine has no pretensions whatever to *originate* anything. It can do whatever we *know how to order it* to perform."[30] This is a pretty mild claim for the animation of matter, not nearly as lurid as Mary Shelley's. The claimant in this case is Ada Augusta, countess of Lovelace, Babbage's disciple, Byron's daughter.

Goldberg's Professor suggests that other tinker, Conrad's "Professor" in *The Secret Agent* who wants to perfect "a really intelligent detonator."[31] He explains his device while a player piano fugally discharges itself. Player pianos, after all, are also self-regulating, though perforated paper for coding data originates in the mechanization of weaving, not music. Babbage adapted the idea from the automatic drawloom of J. M. Jacquard (1801), an adaption that allowed Lady Lovelace to comment floridly, "The

20 *The Bride Stripped Bare* is a painting-construction on glass. A surreal scenario invites occult interpretation, but I want merely to restate the known. Desire in the nine Bachelors (the Malic Moulds, lower left) originates as a gas, is converted into a solid, and then into a liquid in playful chemistry invisible to the eye. As a liquid it is discharged into the domain of the Bride (the insectlike creature, upper left) who responds by taking off invisible clothes. The Bachelors cherish her as Professor Butts cherishes his palm tree: at a distance. Philadelphia Museum of Art: Bequest of Katherine S. Dreier.

Analytical Engine weaves *Algebraic patterns* just as the Jacquard-loom weaves flowers and leaves."[32]

Men and women have always spun yarns: tales and skeins of thread. The Homeric "rhapsodist was literally a 'stitcher of songs.'"[33] Tale-telling knits up the raveled sleeve. Ishmael spins one about the big fish that got away, and we become bodiless beings. Fiction (for a while) overcomes friction. Women have always knit up the raveled sleeve, as if sewing and weaving were ways of undoing time and retying the cord.

6

Before the scientific revolution the world was more like a garment men wore about them than a stage on which they moved. In such a world the convention of perspective was unnecessary. . . . It was as if the observers were themselves *in* the picture.[34]

The Man in the Red Turban in the painting by van Eyck (1433) is the first sitter in Western painting who makes eye contact with the spectator, and Panofsky draws the logical conclusion: that van Eyck is facing a mirror and is the subject of his own reflection.[35]

The Man in the Red Turban steps upon the stage of the world and becomes the object of his own reflection. A mirror offers perspective: our image in it is twice our distance from the glass. As an expression of distance, perspective is an expression of consciousness. The Man in the Red Turban expresses a mythologem of maturity.

In Roman sculpture, unlike Greek, "the faces look back: their eyes engage our eyes. Literacy created a man no longer afraid to use his sight openly: to observe and be observed."[36] The Man in the Red Turban anticipates the Gutenberg Galaxy. He has eyes but no hands: a genitality of sight, a displacement of flesh. Van Eyck stresses scrutiny. He figures passion not in the body but in the convolutions of the turban. As painter and sitter he represesses touch.

21 *The Man in the Red Turban*

Four hundred years later Niepce and Daguerre invented the "mirror with a memory."[37] Daguerreotypy renders immeasurable the distance between our self and our reflection. The camera represses touch as no painter can. "Photography maintains the presentness of the world by accepting our absence from it."[38]

Van Eyck often painted the Christ Child naked in His Mother's lap. His diaper (His attribute!) separates them, but the Babe is dignified and well bred. In Rembrandt's *Abduction of Ganymede*, Zeus, a fearsome eagle, abducts Ganymede, a bawling child. Ganymede loses control and the result resembles a lightning bolt, not Hogarth's "line of beauty." Does Rembrandt's painting illustrate the law of the return of the repressed? In his later work Rembrandt solicited the presence of hand and preserved the character of paint. In the opinion of Gerard de Lairesse (who sat for him) he painted as if with dung.

If Lairesse thought Rembrandt infantile, he would think pathological that modern Italian, whose name (as it happens) I have forgotten, who bottled his shit and exhibited the bottles. *Poverino*! These bottles will find a place alongside "a pale worm in clouded alcohol; a red and green map of Montisert in the seventeenth century; and a trio of rusted tools bound by a funereal ribbon—a spade, a mattock and a pick."[39] I am quoting from a story by Nabokov in which a Russian émigré visits a provincial museum in France and exits in the Soviet Union. He is at once mad and sane even as the museum is an appropriate metaphor of his madness and sanity: at once a spaceship and a time-machine, a panopticon of the unconscious (even as the unconscious is a provincial museum that houses more dross than gold). If you dig with the old map to guide you, you may discover the pale worm in your own vitrines, your own anxieties and bottles.

Nabokov's tools belong in a provincial museum. Duchamp's urinal and wheel do not. These mischievous readymades—consider their calamitous influence upon my poor Italian—are not implements in the archeology of knowledge. They are poetic images. *The Nude Descending a Staircase* is a stylization of cinema, but the readymades are poetic as photographs are, "sudden saliences on the surface of the psyche."[40]

22 *The Abduction of Ganymede*

Nabokov's émigré wanders (as in a labyrinth) from the near space of his psyche ("France") to the deep space ("the Soviet Union"), where he is trapped. Had he wandered into a perspective painting, he might have vanished into a Hole in the Picture.

23 *A Hole in the Picture*

The law of the return of the repressed is a law of feedback. One could say that Modern Painting (i.e., Impressionism) begins with a relaxation of consciousness, a certain relinquishment of perspective. How then shall we regard an Impressionist painting? Up close its armature dissolves into molecules in motion. At a distance that armature stabilizes into molecules at rest. Impressionism creates an ambient viewer with a demon eye for sorting molecules.

Cézanne locates motion in the eye of the beholder, not his foot. You enter the field in front of Mont Sainte-Victoire, wander toward and climb an accessible slope to the peak. Or you seize a patch of paint, then another, and eye-hold by eye-hold climb the sheer face of the picture-surface. Your eye oscillates between narrative and formal occasion. Gabriel always announces the Good News to Mary across a space and often behind a pillar that separates his mystery from hers and suggests that not everything of consequence in a painting is taking place before your very eyes.

Cézanne enters an enveloping space in which objects decompose and planes collapse. Van Eyck achieves a freshness of tender exactitude and re-creates nature as if she were seen for the first time. Cézanne de-creates that nature smudged by five hundred years of hard seeing and restores her preexistent freshness. He tactilizes the world anew and clothes us in the signifiers of Creation.

Freud's first important case study is of Dora who suffered a jumbling of near and deep spaces. Her symptoms (from head to foot) seem a parody of illness: migraine, nervous coughing, loss of vision, labored breathing, hysterical appendicitis, vaginal catarrh, and a periodic limp! Hogarth's *Satire on False Perspective* might suggest her dissociated landscape.

24 *Mont Sainte-Victoire*. Philadelphia Museum of Art. The George W. Elkins Collection.

25 *Satire on False Perspective*

"In the course of a successful treatment, this incoherence, incompleteness, and fragmentariness are progressively transmuted, as facts, events, and memories are brought forward into the forefront of the patient's mind."[41] How successful, then, was Freud with Dora? How successful was David Copperfield with Dora Spenlow, his child bride who died, in Freud's favorite Dickens?

Like Cézanne, Freud forged a ligature between deep space and near and silted in the deepest space of all. Like Freud, Cézanne peeled aside the signified. There aren't any mythologems of maturity among those who sit or lie. Genitality is a convention, like single-point perspective. "Nature," said Cézanne, "is on the inside."

7 The Bride inspires the Bachelors. The Bachelors inspire the Bride. But they are not alone. In the right-hand sector of the lower glass are three large discs, the Oculist Witnesses. They are not just eye witnesses and voyeurs but that audience without which a work of art is not complete. "Now, 'tis true, / I must be here confin'd by you, / Or sent to Naples." The audience sends Prospero to Naples.

How prudent of Duchamp to assure his players an audience! These players and this audience will doubtless inspire one another time out of mind and world without end, happily ever after.

The Metamorphosis of Shit

The sidewalks were full of dogshit in brilliant colors: ocher, umber, Mars yellow, sienna, viridian, ivory black, rose madder.—Donald Barthelme, "The Glass Mountain"

AS Gulliver discovers a Yahoo in every Englishman, Strephon, the naive hero of Swift's scatological verse, discovers a chamber pot in Celia's cabinet.[1] This duplicitous piece of furniture is meant (of course) to fool the eye (fig. 26 and 27). Gulliver's discovery drives him mad, and Swift couldn't do much about the English either, except vex them. Strephon smells his way "through thick and thin," but now Swift could do better: he built two outhouses where the "gentle Goddess *Cloacine* / Receives all Off'rings at her Shrine."[2] The genteel outhouse displaces the impolite chamber pot, but Swift did not expect Houyhnhnms (who evidently do not shit) to displace Yahoos (who very evidently do). The truth of Gulliver's fourth voyage is vexatious indeed—that the civilizing process conceals but cannot erase the anal priority of human beings.[3] We are easily distracted by the elegant facade of Celia's commode. But if we do not smell the truth of her hidden pot, it will require the special effort of an undistracted eye to keep that hidden pot in sight.

Perspective anamorphoses—from the Greek *ana* (again) + *morphe* (shape)—are images that reshape themselves according to your point of view. If that point is along a conventional (i.e., perpendicular) axis, you will doubtless see a genteel image. But if it is along an unconventional (i.e., oblique) axis, you will see an impolite one (see fig. 28). Look directly at Erhard Schön's woodcut *Was Siehst Du?* (1538) and you see a canonical instance of spiritual rebirth, the whale regurgitating Jonah. But hold it at eye level and look at it slantingly from the left and you see a man shitting. Why is he shitting? Because shitting is the bodily archetype of spiritual rebirth insofar as it liberates the body from itself.

Was Siehst Du? is an anal game of concealment and disclosure—all anamorphoses are—in which covert and overt meanings rhyme: a lesson in sublimation, a teasing acknowledgment of anality. Beneath the expelling mouth, the expelling asshole—I say *asshole* as the Anglo-Saxon poet says *nosthyrl* (i.e., nosehole or

26 and **27** "In vain, the Workman shew'd his Wit / With Rings and Hinges counterfeit / To make it seem in this Disguise / A Cabinet to vulgar eyes" (Swift, "The Lady's Dressing Room").

28

nostril). Beneath tiny upright pious Jonah the vast hidden underside of man: the one who squats and shits. It requires, let us say, a special point of view (which Jonah least of all has) to keep this hidden man in sight.[4]

Of Schön's contemporaries and countrymen, Martin Luther kept him most obsessively in sight. "It's as I've often said," Luther told his wife, "I'm like a ripe *dreck* [shit] and the world's like a gigantic *arschloch* [asshole]." But if Luther thought he didn't belong in the world's asshole, he thought the Devil belonged in his.[5] For the Devil is not just the materialized lord of the world and the flesh, but, as Norman O. Brown has argued, the hallucinated displacement of Luther's own anality. Like a quixotic knight of faith, Luther met him in theological combat, daily and strenuous. Doctrine failing to convince, Luther repulsed him with a fart, a turd, or the sight of his naked backside. Once, "having been worsted," the Devil himself "emitted a crepitation of no

small size."[6] But if the Devil was the source of spiritual jeopardy, God was the source of chronic constipation. During one extended period in 1521, Luther's sweaty efforts to move his bowel were not likely to succeed until the fourth or fifth day. He was afflicted by the Lord, he said, so that he might "not be without a relic of the cross."[7]

It is fitting, then, that Luther suffered his spiritual enlightenment on a privy. At the crucial moment, he relinquished the relic of the cross he bore, "was altogether born again and . . . entered paradise itself through open gates."[8]

> These words [said Luther] "just" and "justice of God" were a thunderbolt in my conscience. They soon struck terror in me who heard them. He is just, therefore He punishes. But once when in this terror I was meditating on these words, "the just live by faith," "justice of God," I soon had the

> thought whether we ought to live justified by faith, and God's justice ought to be the salvation of every believer, and soon my soul was revived. Therefore it is God's justice which justifies us and saves us. And these words became a sweeter message for me. This knowledge the Holy Spirit gave me on the privy in the tower.[9]

The historians, however, are less unanimous than the poets about the locus of Luther's revelation, for the phrase "on the privy" is abbreviated in the original. "Auff diss Cl." may signify a cloaca—it may also signify a cell or chapter.[10] Nevertheless, I intend to follow the poets and psychologists—Auden, Brown, Erik Erikson, John Osborne—whose version, at the very least, grasps an imaginative truth. In Luther's testimony as in Schön's woodcut (though Schön is more relaxed and much funnier), a posture of defecation attends a spiritual renewal. Luther, in fact, has just had the revelatory insight of his career as a theologian, and that is why Auden finds the privy an apt place for his revelation. "For excretion is both the primal creative act—every child is the mother of its own feces—and the primal act of revolt and repudiation of the past—what was once good food has become bad dirt and must be got rid of."[11]

Luther experienced an unexpected breakthrough on the privy, and I say *breakthrough* despite the pun I should prefer to avoid in order to remind us of Luther's constipation, that chronic disorder Brown prefers not to mention lest he imply or we infer that "the dynamic of history"—the slow return of the repressed—depends in some way on one man's uncertain peristalsis. Yet how can he suppress it as unmentionably irrelevant in a study of one so fiercely bound to anal impulses? Brown resists Luther's constipation as some of the faithful have resisted the "tower experience."

Luther stayed a ripe shit in the world's asshole for years, awaiting the day of his deliverance. But the world was suffering its own constipation and took its own unpredictable time before relieving itself of its burden. Luther's experience on the privy—like the world's—may be read as an anagram of anal retentiveness and release, and this is how Erikson reads it, but it is not just an anagram of character but of theology too.[12] Luther's discovery, I mean, is a physic of enlightenment; his doctrine is a metaphysic of shitting.

Justification by faith in God precludes the agency of human will: it is, in this sense, a dogma of despair. Human will and good works which may issue therefrom are of no avail because will and works, like world and flesh, belong to the Devil. I do not say a doctrine of justification by faith occurred to Luther because he was constipated; I say his doctrine is a theological analogy of bodily disfunction. Salvation by faith is the doctrine of a man who wants to shit but cannot, whose will to shit is of no avail, who sits anxiously in hope that shit will come like grace itself, that sweeter message, in a breakthrough of unpredictable issuance. We shouldn't disregard the bodily predicate of Lutheran dogma.

A "healthy-minded" theology as William James called it (one less despairing), like a healthy peristalsis (one less costive), acknowledges the virtue of will but surrounds it with necessity. A healthy person wants to shit and then, at a certain moment, must: the sphincter muscles are appropriately (even symbolically) semi-autonomic. If shitting is a consummate pleasure, it is because at a certain moment free will and necessity, what one wants and what one must, precisely coincide. Dante's formula covers the case: "Our peace in Thy will." The act of shitting well momentarily frees the body from (even as that body joyfully succumbs to) its anal curse.

One denies the dialectic of the sphincter—retention/release, retention/release—at one's greatest peril. In *Great Expectations*, for example, Mrs. Gargery takes greatest pleasure in cleaning house with pail and brush, and the insides of Joe and Pip with tar-water. Her deepest impulse is eliminative. Miss Havisham, on the other hand, preserves the past until it turns yellow and black. Her deepest impulse is retentive. Each woman is traumatized—Mrs. Gargery by assault, Miss Havisham by desertion—traumata which are a posteriori explanations of morbid anality.

Lawyer Jaggers tells Pip that no one has ever seen Miss Havisham eat: indeed, she sits in her chair and stores her stool. She denies time, which is to say, she denies shit. But to deny shit, not to eat, is to become shit, to be eaten (as the yellowed wedding cake is eaten by spiders and mice). Like Mrs. Gargery, Miss Havisham dies before her time and her death is particularly apt. Dickens tells us she accidentally catches fire, but the fairy-tale truth is that, like Krook in *Bleak House*, she spontaneously combusts: the very revenge of nature for denying nature.

Miss Havisham is not thoughtful, and her failure to think is analogous to her failure to shit. Were she able to do the one, she might be able to do the other. Rodin's *Thinker*, for example, is doing the one when he might be doing the other (see fig. 29). Auden's insight has a schoolboy charm, and if I remember aright, it's a reading a schoolchild easily makes. Most of us understand deep down and long since what the posture of the Thinker implies. If there is something risible about him, it is because he is thinking when he might be shitting: as if he were doing the wrong thing at the wrong time.

Nevertheless, if thinking is a "special expression of the *tendency to economize*,"[13] then thinking itself is a higher kind of retention, a sublimation for saving shit and making thought of it. Rodin, however, would surely reject this formula—he wants very much to believe that thinking is a natural function of the body. "What makes my *Thinker* think is that he thinks not only with his brain, but with his knitted brow, his distended nostrils and compressed lips, but with every muscle of his arms, back and legs, with his clenched fist and gripping toes."[14] As if to say: his body thought.

Rodin wants to believe—though he doesn't say it—that thinking is a bodily function as natural as shitting. Yet the fact remains that those fists are not clenched and that the Thinker seems absentmindedly apart from (not one with) his body, an archetype of sublimation gone awry in the West. Rodin originally placed him above a sculptural tableau of The Gates of Hell, a tiny figure damned yet judging, in Christ's judgment seat. At the end, Rodin chose him, somewhat larger than life, as the brooding headstone of his grave. Crouched in the position of a man at stool, the Thinker might have heeded an anal voice; instead he heeds and suffers the voice of highest conscience. Unlike Martin Luther, he

29
Rodin was no fool
When he cast his thinker,
Cogitating deeply,
Crouched in the position
Of a man at stool
[Auden, "The Geography
of the House"]
The Rodin Museum
Gift of Jules E. Mastbaum

will never enter paradise through open gates. Unlike a certain Zen master, he will never "attain enlightenment upon hearing the splash of his own turd in the water."[15]

The Thinker exists neither in time nor flesh. He is like a character in a novel that, like most works of narrative art, elides the movements of time and the bowel. In the early satire of Soviet Communism, *We* (1925), Zamyatin reminds us that in the perfect totalitarian polity "nothing *happens*. . . . In the organism of the One State no peristalsis."[16] In that recent satire of Soviet Communism, Zinoviev's *The Yawning Heights* (1979), some architects fail to provide a school with a "shithouse," embracing that "erroneous theory which states that shithouses [unnecessary in the Communist utopia] should be eradicated at the initial stage."[17] In a fantasy of politics, time—a degradation of eternity—may be as noisome as shit—a degradation of spirit. Peristalsis is a process in time. No time, no peristalsis. No peristalsis, no shit.

A free novelist, like an absolute monarch, is an onlie begetter. He can make the johns in his domain disappear at will and offer a tuppence of commonsense in explanation. The narrator of *The Good Soldier*, for instance, puts it this way: "in a novel . . . you take it for granted that the characters have their meals with some regularity."[18] But Cervantes does not take Sancho's meals for granted, and Sancho's own test of the human (as against the enchanted) is whether or not it shits. Joyce in particular gives the lie to tuppence wisdom by acknowledging the persistence of time and shit.

In the morning heaviness of his bowel, Leopold Bloom passes into an outhouse in his garden. This garden is not edenic because, just as Bloom is not fertilizing his earth mother of a wife, he is not fertilizing mother earth. His dung is in the jakes. But Bloom means to reclaim the garden just as—asquat the cuckstool, "Matcham's Masterstroke" in hand—he unconsciously prophesies the repair of his marriage. "*Matcham often thinks of the masterstroke*"—Bloom's will be the appropriation of Stephen as singing master to Molly—"*by which he won the laughing witch who now*."[19] In the disorder of his estate Bloom "takes refuge in the body, the only place in which [he] can still be aware of his own integrity."[20] Nor does his body fail him: "that slight constipation of yesterday quite gone. Hope it's not too big bring on piles again. No, just right. So. Ah! Costive one tabloid of cascara sagrada. Life might be so" (69). Bloom's refuge in the body is "a type of defensive narcissism":[21] less stigmatically, a politics of bodily well-being.

Bloom's integrity is ontological so that if shitting implies a loss of self, reading implies a restitution. Reading in the jakes is a metaphor of eating, a type of feedback that completes a circuit. Bloom reads an old issue of *Titbits* and nominates the bowel he is about to release "Our prize titbit": as if this piece of bowel were in its own right a minor work of art. (In which artistic color? ocher? umber? sienna?) The ingestion of literature prompts its fecal equivalent, and Bloom adjusts the rhythm of his body to the order of his text: "Quietly he read, restraining himself, the first column and, yielding but resisting, began the second. Midway, his last resistance yielding, he allowed his bowels to ease themselves quietly . . ." (69). If he hasn't fertilized his garden or his wife, perhaps he can fertilize himself, invent a story after "Matcham's Masterstroke," for Joyce identifies excretion with creativity—"chamber music," as he elsewhere calls it—and does not forget that excretion comes first. "All the arts," wrote Auden in a pious sentence, "derive from / This ur-act of making, / Private to the artist."[22]

Envying "kindly" the author who earned three pounds thirteen and six, Bloom imagines a scenario of his own. "The king," writes Joyce, "was in his counting-house."[23] Bloom restrains, yields, resists, allows. Lordly and mathematical. In the transformations of Nighttown he becomes King Leopold I, even as in the jakes every man may be king and every king may be kind, and in the benevolence of amnesty release a body from its confinement.

If the first virtue of "Matcham's Masterstroke" is prophetic (it prophesies the repair of Bloom's marriage), the second is heuristic of the body (it regulates Bloom's bowel), and the third is heuristic of the mind (it stimulates his literary imagination). The fourth and last is the virtue beyond which literature outlives its usefulness: "He tore away half the prize story sharply and wiped himself with it" (70). Bloom exits the outhouse thoroughly refreshed, "lightened and cooled in limb," more benevolent than Jehovah who also "walk[ed] in the garden in the cool of the day."

Bloom may sublimate his prize titbit into romantic puffery or he may not, but he would find incomprehensible the rejection of that metamorphic act in the display of nearly naked bowel. More recent artists have been less discreet: as nearly intent on primary process as Bloom on the goddess's "mesial groove."[24] Leaving aside those who merely bottle, or box, I should notice Salvador Dali who glazed his turds into "immaculate, inorganic" objects—*Unspeakable Confessions*[25]—and Piero Manzoni, my favorite *merdista*, who tinned his shit as if it were tuna (see fig. 30). Manzoni signed and numbered the top of each tin as if it were a checkbook, and there are other assurances of authenticity as well. It will not do to force this attractive container, to assert the anal priority beneath the sublimations of parsimony and orderliness. The wit of this work lies in its graciousness, the obliquity of its invitation to eat shit.

30

Eating shit from a tuna tin is like drinking piss from a fountain—Manzoni's invitation irresistibly recalls Duchamp's inverted urinal (fig. 31). Duchamp tried to exhibit the *Fountain* in 1917, but to his chagrin it was hidden behind a screen, as if it really were the bathroom fixture it claimed not to be. As a revolutionary icon,

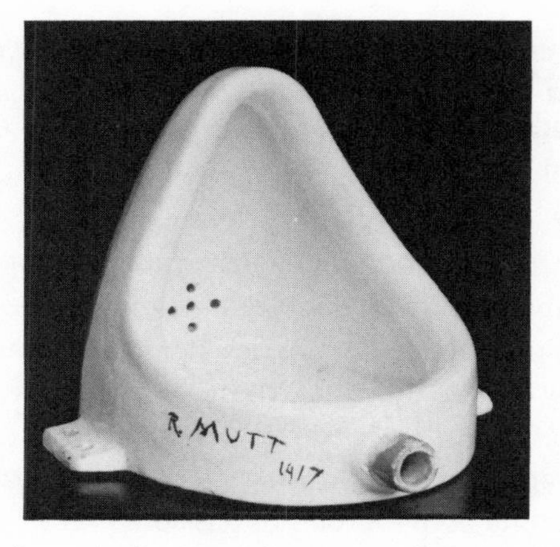

31 Duchamp, *Fountain*. Courtesy Sidney Janis Gallery, New York.

it desecrated two sacred environments: the space of art (the exhibition area) and the space of the body (the torso between throat and anus). Its source, the source of Duchamp's reversal of flow, lies (I think) in the decadence of Huysmans's *Against the Grain*. In the weariness of his days, Des Esseintes discovers "the last aberration from the natural that could be committed," taking anal nourishment through a peptone enema.[26] Waste down the throat, nourishment up the anus: these are the desecrations of the body.

The locus classicus of such inverted activity is *The Hundred and Twenty Days of Sodom* in which the Marquis de Sade revalorizes two commonplace assumptions: that the mouth is the meeting place of the divine and the human (in the ingestion of nourishment and divine nourishment, the consecrated Host) and that the asshole is the meeting place of the human and the demonic (in the gross materiality of shit). *The Hundred and Twenty Days* is an extraordinary exercise in coprophilia. Sadean libertines are connoisseurs of shit. They chew and savor and swallow and wallow in shit. They control the diets of their slaves in order to ensure the aroma and texture of their savory pleasures, and they drink the gurgitations of the enema direct from the assholes of their victims. They are "worshippers" of shit who make a chapel into a privy, a rump into an altar, and the asshole of a victim the depository of a consecrated wafer.

Sade's victims may not shit at will—they must receive (in the author's oddly delicate euphemism) "chapel permission."[27] Shitting without it is a punishable offense: economic victimage, in other words, is as thoroughgoing as sexual and political. These victims are alienated from the means of their bodies' production and from the product of their bodies' labor. They cannot discover their integrity even in the refuge of the body's waste.

The Hundred and Twenty Days is structured according to a "timetable" and proceeds, in Sade's terminology, from simple to complex to criminal to murderous passions—grosser and grosser acts of terrorism and cruelty. Sade finished only one quarter of his novel, the rest is in outline, but that outline—one day/one torture—tells us more truly than any fiction Sade's truest subject: the extenuation of the body in time which most novelists craftily elide and which makes *The Hundred and Twenty Days* such a tedious recital.

"Everything's imaginable," says one libertine, and Sade means to imagine everything sadistic: to totalize it, to immerse us but also himself in fantasies of completion. As, for example, in the twentieth criminal passion: "In order to combine incest, adultery, sodomy and sacrilege, he embuggers his married daughter with a Host" (602). Sade is so intent on the behavior of bodies that he slides into algebraic symbols in the forty-sixth complex passion: "He has girls A and B shit. Then he forces B to eat A's turd, and A to eat B's. Then both A and B shit a second time, he eats both their turds" (579).

In the completed portion of his book—and this was Sade's plan for the whole—a prostitute doubling as a "storyteller" recounts her adventures. Each day she arouses the libertines, and each day they perform the fantasies her exploits inspire. Sade declares his faith in the aphrodisiac of literature, for he means us to perform our fantasies on reading his. The libertines, their slaves, auxiliaries, and staff live—and some die—at a remote and isolated chateau. *The Hundred and Twenty Days*, that is, is a masturbatory daydream bound by a single-minded infliction of pleasure and pain, and that is why "the least display of mirth" is proscribed as "one of the gravest faults" (247). It is mirth, precisely, that results when the pornographic faculty encounters the reality principle: as it does on the eighth day of the murderous passions. Three of the libertines have brutalized a kitchen servant despite her tabooed status in the world of necessary work. "The cooks complain and say that the service will not be able to continue any longer if Messieurs go on fussing with the help" (634).

Sade's unfinished manuscript is itself beset with confessions of vulnerability. There is a self-addressed note after the first part entitled "Mistakes I Have Made"—like rueful mirth, a touching acknowledgment that, even amid hundreds of sadistic exempla, the harshest masters of all are consistency and verisimilitude. The outline of the second part seems to list 151 torments instead of the requisite 150. "Find out why there is one too many," Sade asks himself, for he has inadvertently and comically omitted complex passion number 69, just as Sadean libertines exclude soixante-neuf from their sexual repertoires.

Unlike Uncle Toby who doesn't know the right side of a woman from the wrong, the libertine knows the right but prefers the wrong. Indeed, if anything may be said to disgust him, it is the right side, just as nothing so much as an anal impulse is likely to urge him to an erection. Sade does not explain how the libertine abolishes a disgust for shit, but in the perverse sainthood of that abolition, he becomes an infant again (410). "It was generally proclaimed that all subjects without exception would hereafter never wash themselves, and never under any circumstances wipe the ass after having shitted" (517). The libertine subverts the first discipline of the body, the foundation stone upon which Rabelais (for one, and famously) predicated the civilizing process.

Gargantua's first act of acculturation, in other words, is a denial of shit, the search for a suitable ass wiper. He tries more than fifty devices in a wonderful parody of what we might call scientific research. He tries household objects like cushion and napkin, articles of apparel like neckerchief and coif, plants like gourd leaves and cabbage, animals like hen and pigeon, fibrous products like hay and paper. The one device he does not try, the one that would have signified infantilism instead of maturation, is the one Sadean libertines prefer to any other—the human tongue. Gargantua finally chooses the neck of a well-downed goose and experiences a kind of heavenly bliss ("Do not imagine that the felicity of the heroes and demigods in the Elysian Fields,"[28] etc., etc.). Ass wiping is his first lesson in the economics of exchange: he learns that the exaction of culture is not without its sublime reward. He also learns—a lesser pleasure—that he is a poet, and in that analogous mode of making, he writes a poem about wiping, the subject at hand: "Who his foul bum with paper wipes / Will on his ballocks leave some chips" (67). Not very good, but Gargantua is only five years old.

The end of the civilizing process is Gargantua's construction of the Abbey of Thélème, a utopian community in which there are no privies evident. Its motto is "Do What You Will," though no one seems willing to exercise his lowliest function. Precious stones abound in the architecture of the Abbey and in the clothing of the residents: the spiritualization of shit.

In the period after his discovery of the down-necked goose, Gargantua establishes a routine of daily evacuation. He rises at 4 A.M., hears a chapter of Holy Writ, says his prayers, and then goes "into some private place to make excretion of his natural waste products" (87). Rabelais tells us that in Gargantua's time-bound regimen he does "not waste an hour of the day" (87). I mention this regimen because Gargantua banishes clocks from Thélème, arguing that "the greatest waste of time he knew was the counting of hours—what good does it do?—and the greatest nonsense in the world was to regulate one's life by the sound of a bell, instead of by the promptings of reason and good sense" (150). Since the residents of Thélème are untroubled by evacuation, they can hardly be troubled by evacuatory routine, and, in fact, they order their affairs not by the clock but by chance and opportunity, the promptings of reason and good sense. They are free, equal, accomplished, and virtuous. Doubtless they are happy, though Rabelais never says so. Alas, they do not know the exquisite pleasure of the down-necked goose.

As a prisoner in Lilliput, Gulliver also establishes a routine of daily evacuation. "My constant Practice was, as soon as I rose, to perform that business in open Air, at the full Extent of my Chain" (12). And Gulliver is time-bound too: he "seldom did any Thing without consulting" his watch, "the God that he worships," according to his Lilliputian examiners (18).

Sade did not construct the Chateau of Sillings in answer to the Abbey of Thélème, though it's as if he had. Libertines also do what they will, and if we cannot say they are free or virtuous, rationally or temperately happy, we cannot deny they are exquisitely pleasured. Time-bound in the braces of an infantile ethic, their lives caricature the lost body of childhood. This is the body Gargantua renounces, and that is why *nothing happens* at the Abbey in the life of the flesh. Whereas at the Chateau—most certainly in those long lists of torture—nothing happens except in the flesh.

Gargantua constructs the utopian Abbey of Thélème (in which there is no shit) in answer to the distopian convents and abbeys of France (in which there is nothing but shit). This polarization (like Swift's in Houyhnhnmland) is total, and shit assumes an entirely negative valence. The conventionally doctrinaire "eat the world's excrement, that is to say, sins" without realizing the unpalatability of their diets. "As eaters of excrement they are cast into their privies—their convents and abbeys" (125–26): cesspools of spiritual benightedness. Rabelais cannot reconcile the dignity of Thélème with shit, the mark of a fallen world.

In the fifth book of *Gargantua and Pantagruel* (in a chapter perhaps not authentic) we meet Queen Quintessence who reminds me of that useful anthropological tribe, the Chagga, whose menfolk plug their assholes in quixotic defiance of nature: "When [her masticators] had thoroughly chewed her food, they poured it into her stomach through a funnel of the finest gold. For similar reasons . . . she only sat on the close-stool by proxy" (654). She is a royal person who need never subject herself to the bodily bondage of her subjects. As defiant as any Chagga, she preserves the spurious dignity of office.

Insofar as the closestool raises its sitter above the squat of natural man, it dignifies him, and that is why sometimes (comically and sadly) it is called a throne. For example, in *L'Assommoir* Gervaise visits Coupeau at the asylum of Sainte-Anne and finds him "sitting on this throne, a wooden box affair, very clean and quite odorless. . . . They had a good laugh at her finding him performing, with his bum taking the fresh air. . . . He sat there in majesty, like the Pope himself. . . ."[29] Coupeau tells his wife that he is "quite regular again," and they have "another good laugh, for deep down inside them there was a great joy" (330). In fact, Zola nowhere indicates they ever had greater joy—not even at the outset of their marriage—than they have now, despite Coupeau's alcoholic hallucinations. I think we must attribute half this deep-down joy to his bodily well-being, the other half to his wife's pleasure in his performance.

The further you are from shit (majestically papal or not), the nearer you are to God, which is why the flush toilet is not just an instrument of technological intimidation, a way of intimidating the natives, but of spiritual confirmation, a way of confirming one's spiritual supremacy. Perhaps the modern master of these bitter ironies is the Spanish novelist Juan Goytisolo. I am thinking in particular of *Juan the Landless*.

On the slave island of Semper Fidel, natives watch Master and Mistress atop their double throne—the first flush toilet (as it were) in the New World—shit through slitted clothing. "I have shat like a queen," murmurs Mistress to Master who "celebrates in silence this clear and luminous triumph of the sublimatory occultist technology that further separates the animal from the human. . . ."[30] But what of the divine? "Neither the Redeemer nor the Virgin expelled fecal matter," Goytisolo remarks. Should there have been "visceral eliminations . . . they would have been lovingly preserved by pious souls as precious sacred relics" (11–12). Since there aren't any, we must presume they never existed. Q.E.D. The residua of the blessed are exhaled cutaneously as a sweet refined liquid—Goytisolo quotes St. Bernard four times to this effect. But what of that Spanish king whose exalted person also exhaled aromatic essences, or of Father Vosk who lectures us on resisting creatural urges, or of the blessed child Alvarito, not quite a saint but almost, who resisted those urges so strenuously that the Virgin herself finally crowned his superhuman efforts—and he shat "with neither sound nor fury, in a fragrant and noble manner" (183)? Goytisolo ridicules the metamorphosis of shit into purest spirit and pitilessly contemns the impacted self-delusion of Sunnyspain.

He exhorts us "to a healthy reconciliation with the hidden face of the body and its intimate, extremely personal fruit" (200), though his exhortations (as often as not) are themselves sardonic and contemptuous.[31] He rejects toilet paper as a remnant of Bernardan sophistry. He praises the squat position—medical no less than literary hygienists have praised it as the optimum method for freeing the abdominal muscles—and he encourages a "return to the old, intimate pleasures of emission in common sewer ditches" (188), fraternal shitting in a democratic age.

The long-lived protagonist of Günter Grass's novel *The Flounder* remembers "the horde shit-together" as the "primordially democratic" rite of the Neolithic Age.[32] Horde members (according to this conceit) are phylogenetically infantile: they "identif[y] with [their] feces" (237) and in time of famine eat them without disgust. Grass works an ironic inversion between shitting (social and convivial) and eating (private and silent) just as Luis Buñuel works a surrealist inversion on the same theme in *The Phantom of Liberty*. In that film a young woman (acting as if nothing were untoward) joins a shit-together in the dining-room, then retires to a bathroom for a shameful dinner, alone and in silence.

Fraternal shitting is the commonest denominator of the body politic, and it is upon that denominator that Goytisolo, Grass, and Buñuel practice their comic and desperate ambivalence. The "excrement festival" of *Slaughterhouse-Five*, on the other hand, is not festive at all: collective diarrhea provokes a catatonia of disgust in three Englishmen and a "vision of Hell" in Billy Pilgrim.[33] Vonnegut's satiric phrase, in fact, more precisely describes an anecdote in Carlo Levi's memoir, *Christ Stopped at Eboli*. On Sundays, in that time, eight or ten Italian immigrants would take a train from New York City into the deserted countryside and there "beneath a tree, all of us together would let down our trousers."[34] An excrement festival of very homesick men. "We felt like boys again, as if we were back in Grassano; we were happy, we laughed and we breathed for a moment the air of home" (96). Refuge in the body: the mastery of sphincter muscles, if no other mastery. The rediscovery of childhood, the restoration of community. The reawakening of nationhood, for "when we had finished we shouted together: 'Viva l'Italia!!'" (96). These Italians of an older way disapprove of "American toilets, shiny and all alike." They squat under the tree in reconciliation with the personal fruit of their bodies, for what can the air of home they breathed for a moment be if not the scent of their own fruit?

If the flush toilet encourages the separation of face from ass, reading in the jakes ratifies that encouragement. For reading disguises a low-bodied function with a high-minded one, a necessity

32 Charles I and II may have used—James II certainly used—this handsome closestool.

33

of nature with a luxury of culture. Queen Elizabeth owned one of Harington's flush toilets—Harington owned the other—and the queen kept *The Metamorphosis of Ajax* chained nearby. Her successors were *retardataire* and, book in hand or not, preferred the velvet comfort of the royal cube (fig. 32). Needless to say, they order these things better in France. "Louis XV's smartest stool was in black lacquer with Japanese landscapes and birds in gold and coloured relief, with inlaid borders of mother-of-pearl, Chinese bronze fittings, red lacquer interior, and a padded seat in green velour"—a throne, in fact, for conducting affairs of state.[35] But if the Golden Age of the closestool is Rococo, the Golden Age of the flush toilet—its moment of maximum artistic elaboration—is Victorian. Consider, for example, Thomas Twyford's "Unitas" model of 1883: "Raised Oak" pattern on the outside, blue-and-white floral porcelain underglaze on the inside (fig. 33). Marcel Duchamp turned a garden-variety urinal into an unintentional work of art, but Twyford's toilet is an intentional thing of beauty and use, though I am not comparing it with the *finest* Grecian urns and Chinese vases.

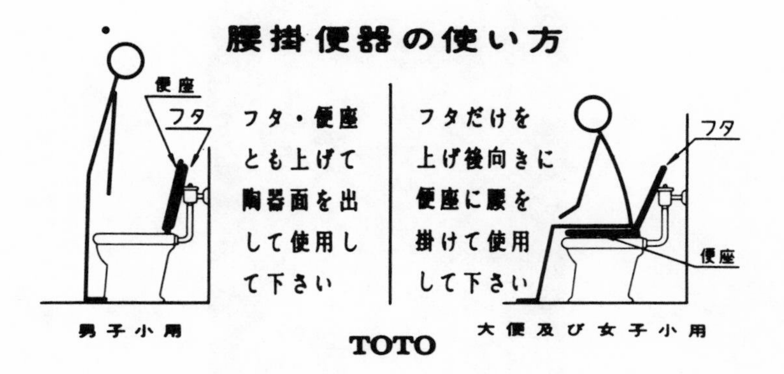

34

Sitting atop the "Unitas" surely signifies a small Faustian triumph, but if squatting is healthier, that triumph is hollow. They order these things better in Japan, where squatting over a hole is received wisdom—or was. Guests at the Tokyo Hilton, unfamiliar with American ways, may have recourse to the stick diagram (fig. 34). Americans, of course, cannot be expected to imitate the manner of the Japanese (even if their clothing permitted) or recreate the manufacture of the Victorians: we use floral deodorants nowadays, not floral underglaze. Perhaps Kenneth Burke is right: that Freud's "death-instinct" is really a "tragic dignification" of an "excretion-instinct," a much less dignifying formula for the body's daily death. In any case, the avoidance of shit seems to be a phobic predicate of our culture.

Freud associated disgust with the smell of feces—the feces of the other, not the self—with the achievement of an upright posture.[36] This posture stylizes anal-erotic repression just as the capacity for disgust (formalized in toilet training) mediates between human and animal. The anal-erotic instinct is not usually prolonged into adulthood with infantile force, least of all in the pure form of a Sadean libertine: coprophage, sodomite, homosexual. Infants, however, are coprophilic, and shit, their most valued product, is eventually projected through a sequence of displacements Ferenczi traced—shit, mud, sand, pretty pebbles, marbles or buttons, shining coins of gold—into the substance men value most.[37]

The anal-erotic instinct, deflected by sublimation (into thrift) or reaction-formation (into cleanliness), lives on in the unconscious and gives life to that equation of startling and apparent contradiction, shit is money. All agricultural communities subscribe to the Chinese proverb "waste is treasure," in which the least valued is the most valued: in this equation, shit is death which gives life, the last which shall be first. Shit carries a very powerful double charge, positive and negative, and that is why it is the body's most magical substance.

This double charge encourages such contradictory notions as: (1) prolonged constipation is autointoxicating; that shit in the body is a poison; and (2) in a mixture with other ingredients—urine, for example—it is a medicine. (Yahoos certainly believe it is a medicine.) But even in more scientifically sophisticated cultures—i.e., our own—we believe that shit, like other bodily discharges, changes from neutral to negative valence on being excreted. The crucial issue, as Mary Douglas has written, is the reduction of dissonance in the preservation of boundary, and she quotes Lord Chesterfield on dirt: "matter out of place," a definition whose archetypal origin must be "shit out of the body."[38] Shit, the first extension of the self, is also the first instancing of the other.

The double charge of shit narrows to single effect in the dramatic testimony of two modern culture heroes, Mahatma Gandhi and Antonin Artaud. Gandhi "spent at least twenty minutes [every morning] squatting on the commode," and every evening he took an enema.[39] Just as he made a practice of "clean[ing] up someone else's excrement," someone else (i.e., a disciple) immediately emptied his chamber pot (52)—an invitation for saints, children, and the surreally inclined. An obsessively cleansed body in an obsessively clean bathroom: rituals of riddance and purification. The machine of the body processes shit in the temple of the bathroom: the fuller the expulsion, the more bounded the body.

Opposite Gandhi is Artaud who wrote "caca is the raw material of the soul."[40] Shit is soul-matter. Loss of shit is loss of soul. The holy man Gandhi is obsessed by wholeness of body. The madman Artaud is anguished by loss of soul. *Kaka* is French for shit, but *ka*—as Artaud knew—is (ancient) Egyptian for soul. The body doubles the soul; shit doubles the body. Artaud's definition of caca is deadly serious but his pun (willy-nilly) is comical—though the last thing his letters from the asylum at Rodez intend is comedy. And least of all belly laughter, the purgative comedy par excellence that inspires Tristram Shandy (for example) to write his book.

> In order, by a more frequent and more convulsive elevation and depression of the diaphragm, and the succussations of the intercostal and abdominal muscles in laughter, to drive the *gall* and other *bitter juices* from the gall-bladder, liver, and sweetbread of his majesty's subjects, with all the inimicitious passions which belong to them, down into their duodenums.[41]

Comic relief (so called) "takes a load off our minds" (it relieves us) as shitting takes a load from our bodies (we relieve ourselves). Laughing and shitting lighten us and confer buoyancy.

The restorative of physiological purging, a comic metaphor in *Tristram Shandy*, is a tragic metaphor in *Oedipus Rex*. In the school of Hippocrates, according to Butcher, catharsis "strictly denotes the removal of a painful or disturbing element from the organism, and hence the purifying of what remains, by the elimination of alien matter."[42] In Aristotle's theory of tragedy, catharsis is a medical metaphor and "denotes a pathological effect on the soul analogous to the effect of medicine on the body" (245). Pity and fear in the tragic spectacle "expel" the painful or disturbing aspect of those emotions in the spectators, affording them pleasurable relief. The homeopathic technique regulates the organism—not permanently, but for a time—and restores it to its normal course.

Oedipus is polluted and Thebes, which has ingested him, is made ill. A purifying of the organism is necessary, and the city does finally eliminate its alien matter, Oedipus himself, the sick man who administers the medicine. But on cathartizing Thebes, Oedipus is also the physician who purifies himself, and the pathological effect of this medicine is the denouement of *Oedipus Rex*. Oedipus takes out his offending eyes, and his fate relieves us of the pity and fear that fate excites.

When Adam ate the apple, part of it stuck in his throat. The Adam's Apple is an unswallowed (hence undigested) piece of fruit, and no matter how well one shits, one can never expel it from the eden of the body it pollutes. We say: an apple a day keeps the doctor away. By which we mean: an apple is a natural purgative that keeps us in bodily health (even if it cannot homeopathically purge the offending fruit). For spiritual sickness we administer a spiritual purgative, confession or psychoanalysis (the "cathartic method" as Freud once thought to call it). Like sick Gargantua, we evacuate at the mouth.

As the Earth is the fallen world at the center of the medieval universe, the dross at the center of the Earth is the center of the Devil, his asshole. Chaucer's Summoner claims friars live there, and there are medieval paintings of Satan ingesting one sinner as another, having passed through his digestive tract, exits below (fig. 35). In the *Inferno* Vergil (with Dante on his back) climbs

35

down the Devil's torso in final descent to Hell's lowest point, "where the huge thighbone / Rides in its socket at the haunch's swell."[43] Vergil and Dante have passed down (if not through) the Devil's body, and now, at his anal point, they reverse direction in obedience to a different gravitational field. They wander through Lethean caverns measureless to man against the flow of the river—from the watery oblivion of an anal birth—till they fetch up beneath Purgatorial stars.[44]

The Devil's domain of sin is the domain of shit, and the Inferno is "one vast excremental dungeon [in which] the air is discolored, the water is syrupy filth . . . the ground is miry, all [is] fetid."[45] All sinners suffer this squalid atmosphere, but Dante reserves a special excremental torment for the destroyers of language, the flatterers of the Eighth Circle:

I,
Thence peering down, saw people in the lake's
Foul bottom, plunged in dung, the which appeared
Like human ordure running from a jakes. (184)

But the Inferno itself is a secure and eternal jakes: it will forever besmear its inhabitants and it will never overflow. The idea of entropy is foreign to Dante's metaphysic.

It is not foreign to the author of *The Confidence-Man* who is also compelled by Last Things. In Melville's final tableau the lights of the Universe dim as dim-eyed Everyman, equipped with money-belt, insurance policy, and counterfeit detector, asks the Con Man what else he needs to be saved. The Confidence Man recommends a life preserver, "a brown stool with a curved tin compartment underneath."[46] Everyman, senile and misguided, accepts the stool with gratitude. The Con Man—at once God and the Devil—complains of a foul odor (!) and extinguishes the last lamp. The Universe has run down and begun to decay. The categories of difference have collapsed.

The principle of entropy holds that energy in a system goes from a greater to a lesser state of differentiation, and it is possible that the curiously flattened style of *The Confidence-Man* reflects this principle, just as the defeated lives of Bouvard and Pécuchet reflect the draft-note with which Flaubert records Pécuchet's sense of final loss: "End of the world because heat runs out."[47] In truth, "everything has come to pieces in their hands" (288), and this image of dissolution (with which Flaubert concludes) reminds us of their greatest triumph. Pécuchet decides to go on a "dung-hunt" one day, and Bouvard, aroused and desiring, falls into a frenzy of manufacture.

> In the compost pit were heaped branches, blood, intestines, feathers, anything he could find. He used Belgian liqueur, Swiss "lizier," washing soda, smoked herrings, seaweed, rags, had guano sent, tried to make it—and carrying his principles to the limit, did not tolerate any waste of urine; he did away with the lavatories. Dead animals were brought into his yard, and used to fertilize his land. Their disembowelled carrion were strewn over the countryside. Bouvard smiled amid all this disinfection. A pump fixed up in a farm cart spread out liquid manure over the crops. If people looked disgusted, he would say: "But it is gold! gold!" (48)

Bouvard very nearly creates shit for its own sake: as if he stood in the vanguard of history and knew it, under the sign of thermodynamic decay.

Bouvard would feel right at home in Bouville, the Mudville of Sartre's *Nausea*. The Confidence Man imagines the world as shit, but in a garden under a chestnut tree, Roquentin suffers that vision: of existence as nauseatingly viscious: soft, sticky, filthy, putrescent. The garden is not Eden, the tree is not an apple, and Roquentin doesn't fall, though it's as if he does in Sartre's adamic metaphor—his consciousness of the chestnut stump "stay[s] there, in [his] eyes, as a lump of food sticks in the wind-pipe."[48] Roquentin watches the "gelatinous slither" mount from earth to sky until he "choke[s] with rage" at the absurdity of his vision: of being as filth [*saleté*] (134). "And then suddenly the park emptied as through a great hole" (134)—existence evacuates itself—and Sartre restores his protagonist to ordinary appearances. As existence precedes essence, diarrhea precedes constipation.

Roquentin's disgust reminds us that the excremental dungeons of our time are no longer inside the earth but on it: the Nazi death camps. Murica wears a chamber pot for a crown in Silone's *Bread and Wine*; Fascist castor oil humiliates the humanness of its victims. But the strategy of the death camps—"excremental assault" Des Pres calls it—is to deny humanness categorically in the totalization of disgust.[49] In Wertmuller's *Seven Beauties*, a man drowns himself in a death camp latrine. In Kosinski's *The Painted Bird* a boy is flung into a cesspool. Chamber pots and laxatives are nothing to absolute defilement: man as shit.

But if (in literature) everything depends upon the spirit of representation, immersion may be comic too: shit not just as shit. In *Death on the Installment Plan*, for instance, a balloonist of "grandiose plans" is "completely submerged" for two hours in a pond of liquid manure:[50] in Céline's good-natured hyperbole, "caked, welded, upholstered with shit" (397). Local farm boys "laughed to split a gut" at his decline and fall—the balloon itself "split[s] with a terrible farting noise" on its next expedition (398–99). "Human laughter," wrote Baudelaire, "is intimately linked with the accident of an ancient Fall, of a debasement both physical and moral."[51] Not all great writers of comedy are scatological, but all great writers of scatology are comic. "All that summer [writes Céline] we had to burn at least ten pots full of benzoin, sandalwood, and eucalyptus" to neutralize the stench of the unclean balloon (397). The condition of man (forever burning benzoin, sandalwood, and eucalyptus) is by nature comic, and a dose of disgust is an ideal antidote to dreams of superiority.

Befoulment, in fact, may even imply renewal: Brecht's Edward II—if not Marlowe's—claims he is renewed by the filth that rains upon him in the cloaca of London Tower.

> Upon my head has fallen for seven hours
> The offal of London.
> But such water hardens my limbs: which are now
> Like cedar wood.
> The stench of excrement gives me boundless greatness![52]

We shall take Edward at his word, remembering the involuntary character of his confinement. Terry Southern, on the other hand, asks for volunteers. In *The Magic Christian*, Guy Grand dumps one million dollars into a heated vat of shit, piss, and blood—enough money to inspire anyone with sufficient fortitude to actualize the alchemical dream: draw gold from dross. We don't know if anyone tries, but the same dream (somewhat refined) fatally tempts Chester and Robinson, the guano hunters of *Lord Jim* and (in an even more refined sense) animates Charles Gould in *Nostromo*: to extract silver from the mines of Castaguana.

Terry Southern named a character in *Dr. Strangelove* Bat Guano, and there are many more victims of name-calling (I'm sure) than I know or remember: Beckett's Krapp and Countess Caca (Molloy's incontinent mother), Voltaire's Cacambo (Candide's valet), Gogol's Akaky Akakavitch, Dickens's Mr. Merdle and Mr. Murdstone, Dostoyevsky's Smerdyakov, Svevo's Dr. Coprosich, Smollett's Humphry *Clinker* (fecal deposit), Sterne's Hafen Slakenbergius (chamber pot and pile of shit), Carlyle's Teufelsdröckh (Devil's shit).[53]

Molloy himself is an anal sport who has never renounced an infantile fantasy of anal birth: "of her who brought me into this world, through the hole in her arse if my memory is correct. First taste of the shit."[54] As he lies abed in "the tranquillity of decomposition," he remembers the woman who first "acquainted [him] with love," Ruth—or was it Edith? And he remembers that she put him into the "slit" between her legs—or was it her rectum? This question perturbs Molloy as a matter of romantic doctrine: "Is it true love, in the rectum?" (57). "Love has pitched his mansion in the place of excrement": does Crazy Jane also mean that Love has blackened himself in the asshole of his lover? Perhaps it *was* true love, after all.[55]

"We underestimate this little hole," says Molloy, "we call it the arsehole and affect to despise it. But is it not rather the true portal of our being and the celebrated mouth no more than the kitchen-door?" (80). Molloy's deepest absorption is in his body: sucking stones, counting farts. "Your papers!" cries a suspicious policeman, but, like an infant, Molloy carries no identification papers—only toilet papers. His deepest attachment is not to any Ruth or Edith but to his mother: "I piss and shit in her pot" (7). Now he lies abed, composing and decomposing: a lesser and lessening attachment. Composition for Molloy is like his arsehole, "a link between me and the other excrement" (80).

As Molloy fantasies anal birth into life, Malone fantasies vaginal birth into death. "The feet are clear already, of the great cunt of existence."[56] *Malone Dies*, which follows *Molloy*, condenses the wisdom of its predecessor: "What matters is to eat and excrete" (185). In the elementary town Malone lies abed, not sure he is alive or dead. He has one pot for eating, one for shitting, but now that he has stopped eating, he is filling both pots with shit. Like Moran, Molloy's double from the town of Turdy, Malone knows that "all language [is] an excess of language."[57] He gradually voids himself of the human and dies in a broken trail of words.

The final volume of Beckett's trilogy is *The Unnameable*, which tells of an ancient mutilated creature who lives in a jar, dantesquely punished for having been born. The Unnameable is condemned to talk, to register consciousness as if electro-encephalographically, and to weep, to void tears unceasingly. Molloy and Malone are anally regressive, but the Unnameable is below anality. Tears are an infantile product even more fluxive than shit. (The terminology of flux and void, of course, is both physiological and cosmological.)

The Unnameable attends to First Things and Last. As *kaka* and *ka*, shit and soul, make a folk etymological pun, so do scatology and eschatology, Twain's *1601* and Kubrick's *2001*. But *flatus* (gas generated in the stomach: as in *flatulence*) and *afflatus* (a creative impulse: as in divine *afflatus*) are from the same root, the Latin *flare*, to blow. As above, so below. Luther's seizure on the privy makes perfect etymological sense. Martin was lightened and enlightened at the same time.

Appendix: Excremental Language

When a deer in a glade observes a stalking leopard, terror registers in its brain stem: its body grows rigid, its heart beats faster, it voids its bowel. These instinctual responses are "survival mechanisms": the deer shits in order to run faster.

"Mild fear produces constipation, while terror produces diarrhea"[58] in men and deer, though the spirit of diarrheic terror ranges from the comic (as in Aristophanes) to the horrific (as in Hemingway). In *The Frogs*, for example, Aeacus so terrifies Dionysus with the prospect of hellish torment that Dionysus shits—or seems to shit—on stage. His servant, Xanthius, denounces him as cowardly, for cortical thinking regards shitting in terror not as an instinctual response to which no obloquy attaches—a mechanism useful in animals but useless in men—but as an act of cowardice unworthy of a god or man.[59]

In one of the vignettes in *In Our Time* a prisoner about to be executed shits uncontrollably. "Be a man, my son," a priest encourages, but Sam Cardinalla fails (as we say) to die like a man.[60] The guards who carry him to the gallows are, like Xanthius, disgusted. Sam, of course, is humiliated, for a prisoner's last and special triumph is to walk to the noose on his own. He wants to believe—and wants us to believe—that he is not dying (as we say) like a dog. On the other hand, man is the only creature in the kingdom who conspires with his executioner.

A dog or fox may mark his turf by the judicious dropping of odorous dung, and a burglar may announce his presence by giving a shit (i.e., leaving an infantile "gift") at the scene of his crime. His primary motive, in this view, is not contempt but confession, his gift, according to one French criminologist, a "carte de visite odorante."[61] According to Jean Genet his motive is apotropaic: "This familiar act restores his assurance. He knows that in French slang a turd is known as a 'watchman.'"[62] These excremental communiqués, animal and criminal, are invocations against trespass, assertions of territorial imperative.

Norman Mailer is a kind of modern haruspex, an inspector of entrails, who, in "The Metaphysics of the Belly," recommends an actual inspection of bowel: "Because feces are the material evidence of the processes of communication within us."[63] Mailer contends that shit—for whoso can read it—discloses the desire of the cells to the self, and Mailer's life is doubtless rich with inner episode: "When we have communicated nicely within ourselves, the stool reflects a simple reasonable operation (cowflop is, for example, modest in its odor) but where we have failed . . . the odors and shapes are tortured, corrupt, rich, fascinating (that is attractive and repulsive at the same time), theatrical, even tragic" (291)."[64] Mailer confers a literary language upon shit as others confer an excremental language upon literature. At one extreme the production of texts is logorrheic, an "enormous stool of words" as William Gass describes the oeuvre of Henry Miller.[65] At the other it is aphoristic, as in the "foul" epigrams of Robert Herrick, the parsimony of an anal mode.[66] Between catharsis and constipation we may locate the messiness of Dickens, Orwell's celebrator of waste, oranges and halfpence (as in *Dombey and Son*) falling from his coach; and the precision of Flaubert, whose *Temptation of St. Anthony* his friend Bouilhet called a "diarrhea of pearls."

The Museum,
My Home Away from Home

I do not believe that a bit of wafer and a few drops of wine become Christ's Body and Blood in the Mass, but I do believe something no less magical: that a pile of shit in the street becomes a work of art in a museum. If art has done nothing else in this century, it has endlessly challenged the threshold of its religion. So that if the shit has not yet been deposited, it soon will be. And when it is, curators will rise to validate it. Here is a little anthology of phrases they will use:

techniques of the body
history of disgust
origins of making
soft sculpture (Oldenberg)
piles of dirt (Robert Morris)
the blinking hemorrhoid of Nathanael West (*A Cool Million*)

I am not of course judging the quality of the pile of shit as sculpture, only of its being as art, just as, in Malraux's famous example, medieval man did not think of a Romanesque crucifix as sculpture, only as the Christ. You can see then why I'm in a bad way: I'm a true believer in the religion of art.

It's nothing nowadays to pay lip service. "Seventy-nine percent of the museum-goers of the popular classes," according to a statistic I have at hand, "associate the museum with the image of a church."[1] For these visitors the museum is a place of solemnity, and they might well agree with those more sophisticated folk who suppose it a House of the Dead: necropolis, cemetery, dead-letter office, old-age home.[2] (The list grows wittier.) Marinetti wanted to divert the Arno so that it would flow through the Uffizi, not alongside it, but if the dead were really dead, there would be no need to drown them. Monet visited the Louvre in order to turn his back on the paintings,[3] but his contempt is like Tom Sawyer's whistling through the graveyard. The museum is a place of power, not just a dead hand of the past: a House of the Undead.

It is a place of magical danger in Nabokov's story "The Visit to the Museum," in which a Russian émigré passes through an unexpected door into an unimagined world: costumes, books, ancient sculpture, oriental tapestries, marine remains, a planetarium, locomotive machinery, musical instruments, fountains, a greenhouse, chemistry labs. And thence into the Soviet Union. The museum is a time machine and a space capsule as wonderful as any rocketship to outer space. The rooms at Montisert are chambers of wonder, and to pass through them is to live dangerously.

If you can't tell capitalist from communist from the moon, can you tell Bouguereau from Cézanne? (See Note, below).

1. The Metropolitan has permanently installed its Bouguereaus.
2. We have seen the province of Earth from the Moon.
3. Has the Metropolitan become a provincial museum?

I am speaking of quality now, not being, but it is the magical character of an art museum that whatever crosses its threshold can never uncross it. Not even a pile of dirt. A museum is more unyielding than Heaven (from whence Lucifer fell) or Hell (which Christ harrowed); what goes into it never comes out. The Bouguereaus were waiting in the basement. Once a work of art always a work of art.

Once upon a time the Church was patron, and paintings were made for churches. Now the museum is patron in the sense that the large and uninflected surfaces of Hard Edge and Minimal Art, which hardly fit or befit one's private chapel, seem made for the impersonal surfaces of museums. These paintings were made, you may say, from the expectations of Art History, even as the spiral-form of the Guggenheim roughly parodies the continuous space of that history. The Guggenheim defines itself as a Museum of Non-Objective Art, and its design best serves a kind of painting which excludes private delectation. In fact, you have to work hard, nowhere harder, not to tarnish ten paintings at once, and I am reminded of a character in Virginia Woolf who perfects a method for the preservation of freshness. She takes a painting by surprise, sidling up to it and closing her eyes; opening them, she sees the painting, as it were, for the first time. She makes the public communion in which the Guggenheim specializes into a private ritual.

The most spectacular realization of public art as private ritual is the Duchamp enclave at the Philadelphia Museum of Art—the *Etant Donnés* which was literally made for (i.e., built into) the museum that houses it, just as the *Ghent Altarpiece* was made for a certain chapel in a certain church. We approach a large wooden door on which there are two metal discs, behind which are two peepholes, through which only one person at a time may peep. A *tableau vivant* of pornographic violence greets me, but perhaps nothing else in our time is likely to fill me so fully on the instant. Suddenly a voyeur, I am filled with guilt (i.e., religion). My relation to the tableau is a paradigm of confession, and I am ready to confess. Indeed, I am already confessing.

The art museum is a magical place that wants to be a logical place. "Objects in a museum should be illumined by scholastic ordering in their installation. They should be displayed in the light of modern scholarship. A museum should not be a public playground."[4] The art historian Richard Offner pronounced these austere imperatives—at once testamental and taxonomic—in 1927, and certainly "scholastic ordering"—by chronology, style, birthright—has carried the day. Offner believed that a museum "is primarily for scholars," and there is no doubt that as he proclaimed the truth as he saw it, he was also defending his own professional interest, for no one has a greater investment in "scholastic ordering" than an art historian.[5]

In any case, since we classify stars and starlings, why not paintings too? Systems of classification allow us to organize the attributes of objects: thence to construct histories and define schools. The problem is not just that these systems become the frames of reference through which we may see but that, like the frame of an eyeglass, they become the frames without which we can hardly see at all. It is arguable, for example, that Giorgio Morandi (1890–1964) was the finest Italian painter since the elder Tiepolo. Nevertheless, he was not a Futurist (like Boccioni), an Expressionist (like Modigliani), or a Surrealist (like de Chirico). He looks old-fashioned through modish spectacles. We will look—almost in vain—for examples of his work on the walls of our major museums.

It's bad enough that most works on display are displaced from their original (religious, social, political) contexts. It's even worse that scholars cannot resist placing them in academic contexts: historical and stylistic. Scholastic ordering in matters of history and style—Cubist paintings in one place, Italian Primitives in another—is a technique of domestication, and a painting in a museum (with its cousins and confreres) is like an animal in a zoo. No wonder the Fauves look like pussycats now, and only a most remarkable painter (like Cézanne) can retain his wildness. Dioramas—fake contexts—are simply silly. A sculpture in the fake townhouse of the Lehman Collection at the Metropolitan is like a stuffed animal in the Museum of Natural History. Taxonomy and taxidermy are defenses against wildness.

The impulse toward scholastic ordering dates from the emergence of the public museum in the second half of the eighteenth century: it became a way of exercising control not only over works of art and the sensibilities of spectators but over their bodies as well. *For their own good, needless to say.*

> At an exhibition held in the newly opened Zeughaus in Berlin in 1844 it was decided to guide the public along a predetermined route through the galleries, so that they should see everything in the correct order and miss nothing. The design of the building made it difficult to achieve this by notices and

> sequences of doors and corridors, so the visitors were moved along in the right direction by means of spoken or shouted commands, in proper Prussian military fashion.[6]

This musemeological dream of reason produces monsters. No one will miss the pathology of repression in the cause of culture, the herding of subject populations, the prefiguring of a final solution. It is perhaps not so odd, then, that William Morris prophesied the withering away of the museum, that storehouse of alienated objects, in the new age:[7] as if it were the capitalist state itself, a gross tumor of self-aggrandizement.

Let us have a museum that acknowledges a playful interface between objects—a chemistry lab and a greenhouse, a Cubist collage and an Italian Primitive—and we shall make our own contexts or not make them. (The interface between divergent paintings naturally and more nearly occurs in once-private residences like the Frick than at such halfway houses or foster homes as the Museum of Modern Art.) Ishmael taxonomizes whales by folio and duodecimo, but his system is a fable because it fails to admit the existence of nature: the living whale. Ishmael tells the tale of his ignorance, and Moby Dick remains sphinxlike, a hermetic image. And that is what painted images also are—despite the pretense of scholastic ordering—that row of Rembrandts no less than the dematerializations of Conceptual Art.

> The set of objects the Museum displays is sustained only by the fiction that they somehow constitute a coherent representational universe. The fiction is that a repeated metonymic displacement of fragment for totality, label to object, series of objects to series of labels, can still produce a representation which is somehow adequate to a nonlinguistic universe. Such a fiction is the result of an uncritical belief in the notion that ordering and classifying, that is to say, the spatial juxtaposition of fragments, can produce a representational understanding of the world.[8]

I am quoting Eugenio Donato on *Bouvard and Pécuchet* whose protagonists collect bric-a-brac until "their house looked like a museum"—though a museum without discernible sequence.[9] One jumbled room, for instance, contains old books, a genealogical tree, two pastel portraits, a black felt sombrero, a monstrous clog, the remains of a bird's nest, two coconuts, a barrel, and a straw basket with a coin in it. Douglas Crimp argues that the hybrid discontinuity of Robert Rauschenberg's art is the Postmodernist type of the museum, but long before the letter (and long before Nabokov) Flaubert was already parodying the idea of the museum as an assemblage.[10] Furthermore, only the slow rate of decomposition separates one Flaubertian jumble from another, the compost pit Bouvard enthusiastically heaps: blood, feathers, liqueur, washing soda, seaweed, etc. Bouvard makes shit with an artist's pride in the transformation of matter. "If people looked disgusted he would say: 'But it is gold! gold!' "[11] So that to the little anthology of relevant phrases with which I began we may add another:

the compost pit of Gustave Flaubert (*Bouvard and Pécuchet*)

A Note On How You Can Know Cézanne from Bouguereau

The Metropolitan Museum has newly installed its nineteenth-century European paintings in a large well-lit room in the oblong center of which hang the Impressionists and post-Impressionists (including Cézanne). The meaning of this installation is symbolic: Impressionism and post-Impressionism are perceived as the culminating achievements of nineteenth-century European painting and historically central to what comes next. Nor are these judgments subversive.

Along one side of this oblong space there is a broad avenue, equally well lit, for earlier masters—David, Ingres, Goya, Delacroix, Constable, Turner, Courbet. The passage between avenue and centrum is wide, and the partition between them does not reach the ceiling. These earlier masters (the Met is now reminding us) bore a vital relation to those who came after. No confining wall here. And, after all, didn't Renoir consult Ingres? Cézanne, Delacroix? Isn't Turner, and even late Goya, prefigurative of Impressionism? And so on.

At the end of this long avenue—behind rooms devoted to Corot, Millet, and certain popular and academic painters like Bonheur and Cot—there is a shorter hallway which joins this avenue with its opposite on the other side of the oblong. The hallway itself is inhospitably lit and the paintings themselves dimly spot lit. Here, where the bathrooms are, behind a real wall (not a partition), consigned to near and outer darkness, you will find Bouguereau. This is the Met's sly way of encouraging you not to linger before paintings of which it does not approve but which, in this wearying Postmodernist age, it feels obliged to hang. Dim light, dim artistic achievement.

At the other shorter end are two rooms devoted to Degas: rooms of a more uniform, not at all spotty, dimness. Fortunately, a sign (twice posted) explains this dimness—lest we confuse dimness with dimness—and invites our appreciation: "The light in the following two galleries is reduced in order to protect the works of art on paper. Please allow your eyes to adjust to the lower light level." So it isn't very hard, after all, to tell which are the more important paintings and which are the less. And that's how you can know / Cézanne from Bouguereau.

Notes

The American Fix

1 From Oldenburg, *Store Days*, quoted in *Pop Art Redefined*, ed. John Russell and Suzi Gablik (New York: Frederick A. Praeger, 1969), p. 99. This book contains an anthology of writings and interviews by many Pop artists.
2 Quoted in Kenneth Coutts-Smith, *Dada* (London and New York: Studio Vista/Dutton, 1970), p. 23.
3 Quoted in Roland Penrose, *Picasso* (New York: Schocken, 1962), p. 125.
4 Quoted in Russell and Gablik, *Pop Art Redefined*, p. 80.
5 Quoted in Calvin Tomkins, *The Bride and the Bachelors* (New York: Viking Press, 1965), p. 18.
6 Quoted in Russell and Gablik, *Pop Art Redefined*, p. 116.
7 Quoted in Tomkins, *The Bride and the Bachelors*, p. 68.
8 Quoted in Christopher Finch, *Pop Art* (London and New York: Studio Vista/Dutton, 1968), p. 51.
9 Quoted in Russell and Gablik, *Pop Art Redefined*, p. 92.
10 See Jonas Mekas, "The Filmography of Andy Warhol," in John Coplans, *Andy Warhol* (Greenwich, Conn.: New York Graphic Society, 1970).
11 From Tzara, *New York Dada*, quoted in Coutts-Smith, *Dada*, p. 69.
12 Quoted in Russell and Gablik, *Pop Art Redefined*, p. 62.
13 William Rubin, *Dada, Surrealism, and Their Heritage* (New York: H. N. Abrams, 1968), p. 19.
14 Quoted in Tomkins, *The Bride and the Bachelors*, p. 47.
15 Pierre Cabanne, *Dialogues with Marcel Duchamp*, trans. Ron Padgett (New York: Viking Press, 1971), p. 71.
16 From "Apropos of 'Readymades,'" quoted in Coutts-Smith, *Dada*, p. 55.
17 Quoted in Arturo Schwarz, *The Complete Works of Marcel Duchamp* (New York: H. N. Abrams, 1969), p. 144.
18 Quoted in Tomkins, *The Bride and the Bachelors*, p. 66.
19 I draw the language of the drug trip from a glossary compiled by Dr. William D. Alsever, *Ethos* 4, no. 27 (1971).

In Labyrinths

1 W. H. Auden, "The Guilty Vicarage," in *The Dyer's Hand* (New York: Random House, 1968), p. 154.
2 "The Purloined Letter," in *Selected Writings of Edgar Allan Poe*, ed. Edward H. Davidson (Boston: Houghton Mifflin, 1956), p. 212. Subsequent page references to this tale are noted in the essay. Whenever I quote a text more than once, I will follow this manner of citation.
3 James, *The Sacred Fount* (London: Macmillan, 1923), p. 52.
4 James, *What Maisie Knew* (Garden City, N.Y.: Doubleday, 1954), p. 28.
5 W. L. Hildburgh, "The Place of Confusion and Indeterminability in Mazes and Maze-Dances," *Folk-Lore* 56 (March 1945):188–92. See also W. F. Jackson Knight, *Cumaean Gates* (Oxford: B. Blackwell, 1936), pp. 84–89, and Gerardus van der Leeuw, *Sacred and Profane Beauty*, trans. David E. Green (New York: Holt, Rinehart and Winston, 1963), pp. 44–48 for labyrinth dances.
6 James, *The Spoils of Poynton* (Harmondsworth, England: Penguin Books, 1981), p. 135.
7 Poe, *The Narrative of Arthur Gordon Pym* (New York: Hill and Wang, 1960), p. 198 (italics removed). For the resemblance between chasms and initials, see, for instance, John Irwin, *American Hieroglyphics* (New Haven: Yale University Press, 1980), p. 228. Maisie becomes mazy but eap is (and always was) an untranslatable hieroglyph.
8 Robert Lebel, *Marcel Duchamp*, trans. from the French by George Heard Hamilton (New York: Grossman Publishers, 1959), p. 39.
9 Quoted in Arturo Schwarz, *The Complete Works of Marcel Duchamp* (New York: H. N. Abrams, 1969), p. 201.
10 Mark Twain, *Tom Sawyer Detective* (New York: Scholastic Books Services, 1968), pp. 10–11.
11 Mark Twain, *The Adventures of Tom Sawyer* (Harmondsworth, England: Penguin Books, 1971), p. 155.
12 Philip E. Slater, *The Glory of Hera* (Boston: Beacon Press, 1971), p. 391. See also Norman O. Brown, *Love's Body* (New York: Random House, 1968), chap. 2.
13 *Picasso on Art*, ed. Dore Ashton (New York: Viking Press, 1972), p. 159.
14 Borges, *Dreamtigers*, trans. from the Spanish by Mildred Boyer and Harold Morland (New York: Dutton, 1970), p. 93.
15 Paolo Graziosi, *Paleolithic Art*, trans. from the Italian (London: Faber and Faber, 1960), p. 17.
16 For the metaphysics of the threshold, see Angus Fletcher, "'Positive Negation': Threshold, Sequence, and Personification in Coleridge," in *New Perspectives in Coleridge and Wordsworth*, ed. Geoffrey Hartman (New York: Columbia University Press, 1972), pp. 133–64.

17 G. R. Levy, *The Gate of Horn* (London: Faber and Faber, 1948), p. 20.
18 John Layard, "Maze-Dances and the Ritual of the Labyrinth in Malekula," *Folk-Lore* (London) 47 (June 1936):139–70. See also Mircea Eliade, *Rites and Symbols of Initiation*, trans. from the French by Willard R. Trask (New York: Harper and Row, 1965), p. 62.
19 W. H. Matthews, *Mazes and Labyrinths* (New York: Dover, 1970), pp. 66–67.
20 For Spenser's use of the labyrinth, see Angus Fletcher, *The Prophetic Moment* (Chicago: University of Chicago Press, 1971), chap. 2.
21 Brigid Brophy, *Don't Never Forget* (New York: Holt, Rinehart and Winston, 1966), p. 99.
22 Johan Huizinga, *Homo Ludens*, trans. from the German (Boston: Beacon Press, 1955), p. 108.
23 *The Earliest English Poems*, trans. Michael Alexander (Harmondsworth, England: Penguin Books, 1966), p. 99.
24 *The Bride Stripped Bare by Her Bachelors, Even*, a typographic version by Richard Hamilton of Marcel Duchamp's Green Box; trans. George Heard Hamilton (New York: J. Rietman, 1976).
25 James, Preface to *The Golden Bowl* (London: Macmillan, 1923), 1:xx.
26 Knight, *Cumaean Gates*, p. 162.
27 Hammett, *Red Harvest* (New York: Vintage Books, 1972), p. 39.
28 Brophy, *Don't Never Forget*, p. 98.
29 For the relationship of the detective story to the comedy of manners, see George Grella, "Murder and Manners: The Formal Detective Novel," *Novel* 4 (1970–71):30–48.
30 Matthews, *Mazes and Labyrinths*, p. 57.
31 Robbe-Grillet, *In the Labyrinth*, trans. from the French by Richard Howard (New York: Grove Press, 1965).
32 Camus, "The Minotaur, or The Stop in Oran," in *The Myth of Sisyphus*, trans. from the French by Justin O'Brien (New York: Knopf, 1959), pp. 114–33.
33 Kafka, *The Castle*, trans. from the German by Willa and Edwin Muir (New York: Modern Library, 1969), p. 14.
34 Lewis Carroll, *The Annotated Alice*, ed. Martin Gardner (New York: C. N. Potter, 1960), p. 199.
35 Barth, "Lost in the Funhouse," in *Lost in the Funhouse* (New York: Grosset and Dunlap, 1971), p. 97.
36 Borges, "Death and the Compass," in *Labyrinths*, trans. from the Spanish by Donald A. Yates and James E. Irby (New York: New Directions, 1964), p. 86.
37 Melville, *Moby-Dick*, ed. Charles Feidelson, Jr. (Indianapolis: Bobbs-Merrill, 1964), p. 267.

Charles Olson: Obeying the Figures of the Present Dance

1 I have used the following abbreviations in citing Olson's titles in my text: HU—*Human Universe and Other Essays*, ed. Donald Allen (New York: Grove Press, 1967); CMI—*Call Me Ishmael* (New York: Grove Press, 1958); M—*The Maximus Poems* (New York: Jargon/Corinth, 1960); SW—*Selected Writings*, ed. Robert Creeley (New York: New Directions, 1966); AM—*Archeologist of Morning* (London: Cape Goliard Press, 1970); SVH—*The Special View of History* (Berkeley: Oyez, 1970); BOA—*A Bibliography on America for Ed Dorn* (San Francisco: Four Seasons Foundation, 1964).
2 Ann Charters, *Olson/Melville* (Berkeley: Oyez, 1968), p. 64. Hereafter referred to as OM.
3 Herman Melville, "Hawthorne and His Mosses," reprinted in *The Shock of Recognition*, ed. Edmund Wilson (New York: Doubleday, 1943), 1:193–94.
4 "Letters for Origin," ed. Albert Glover (Ph.D. diss., SUNY/Buffalo, 1968), p. 76. Hereafter referred to as LO. I have tried to reproduce or at least approximate wherever relevant Olson's typography, spacing, and punctuation—"the spatial proportions of the original letters" in Glover's phrase. I have drawn my quotations from this manuscript because the published edition (*Letters for Origin, 1950–1960*, ed. Albert Glover [London: Cape Goliard Press and New York: Grossman Publishers, 1970]) is a selection that does not always include the letters or parts thereof I quote.
5 Robert Duncan, "Notes on Poetics Regarding Olson's *Maximus*," *Black Mountain Review*, no. 6 (1956):202.
6 Herman Melville, *Pierre* (New York: Grove Press, 1957), p. 476.
7 Herman Melville, *Moby-Dick*, ed. Charles Feidelson, Jr. (Indianapolis: Bobbs-Merrill, 1964), p. 549.
8 George Butterick, *A Guide to the Maximus Poems of Charles Olson* (Berkeley: University of California Press, 1978), p. 92.
9 John Finch, "Dancer and Clerk," *Massachusetts Review* 12, no. 1 (1971): 34–40.
10 Charles Olson, "A Syllabary for a Dancer," *Maps*, no. 4 (1971):9–15.
11 Martin L. Pops, *The Melville Archetype* (Kent, Ohio: Kent State University Press, 1970).

Sleeping Beauty Spurned: Remarks on Modern and Postmodern Dance

1 Doris Humphrey, *The Art of Making Dances*, ed. Barbara Pollock (New York: Holt, Rinehart and Winston, 1959), p. 15.
2 Gaston Vuillier, *A History of Dancing* (New York: D. Appleton, 1898), p. 77.
3 Isadora Duncan, *The Art of the Dance*, ed. Sheldon Cheney (New York: Theatre Arts Books, 1928), p. 48.

4 James J. Corbett, *The Roar of the Crowd* (New York: Arno Press, 1976), p. 269.
5 John Martin, "Isadora Duncan and Basic Dance," in *Nijinsky, Pavlova, Duncan*, ed. Paul Magriel (New York: Da Capo Press, 1977), p. 5.
6 Corbett, *The Roar of the Crowd*, p. 269.
7 Stéphane Mallarmé, "Ballets," in *Mallarmé*, trans. from the French by Bradford Cook (Baltimore: Johns Hopkins University Press, 1956), p. 61.
8 Isadora Duncan, *My Life* (New York: Boni and Liveright, 1927), p. 95.
9 Graham, "A Modern Dancer's Primer for Action," in *Dance As a Theatre Art*, ed. Selma Jeanne Cohen (New York: Dodd, Mead, 1974), p. 136.
10 Joseph H. Mazo, *Prime Movers* (New York: William Morrow, 1977), p. 204.
11 Sally Banes, *Terpsichore in Sneakers* (Boston: Houghton Mifflin, 1980), p. 24.
12 Duncan, *The Art of the Dance*, p. 96.
13 Henry Adams, "The Dynamo and the Virgin," in *The Education of Henry Adams* (Boston: Houghton Mifflin, 1918), pp. 383, 385.
14 Olga Maynard, *American Modern Dancers* (Boston: Little, Brown, 1965), p. 31. Adams had, in fact, admired bare-breasted dancing girls in Samoa in 1890. He thought they were (as Isadora thought herself) avatars of the Greek: "You can imagine the best female figure you ever saw, on about a six foot scale, neck, breast, back, arms and legs, all absolutely Greek in modelling and action, with such freedom of muscle and motion as the Greeks themselves hardly knew . . ." (see Carlos Baker, "Moralist and Hedonist: Emerson, Henry Adams, and the Dance," *New England Quarterly* 52, no. 33 [1979]).
15 Cited in Maynard, *American Modern Dancers*, p. 66.
16 *New York Times*, February 17, 1980, sect. 2, p. 7.
17 Arlene Croce, *After-Images* (New York: Vintage Books, 1979), p. 52.
18 Duncan, *The Art of the Dance*, p. 112.
19 In *Huddle* several people group themselves as in a football huddle; one, detaching himself, climbs up and over the bodies of his colleagues and finds a place on the other side. Then it is someone else's turn.
20 Banes, *Terpsichore*, pp. 41–43.
21 Yvonne Rainer, *Work 1961–73* (New York: New York University Press, 1974), p. 51.
22 Rainer, "Statement: for *The Mind is a Muscle*" in ibid., p. 71. Rainer's task-dance *Room Service* requires three teams of three members each to clamber upon and over various paraphernalia in a follow-the-leader fashion. Its deeper task is to unmask the dancers of their stage presence.
23 Arthur Knight, "Cine-Dance," *Dance Perspectives* 30 (Summer 1967):5.
24 Quoted in Allan Kaprow, *Assemblage, Environments & Happenings* (New York: H. N. Abrams, 1966), p. 195.
25 Murray Louis, "Foreward Is Not Always Going Ahead," *Dance Perspectives* 38 (Summer 1969):32–33.

26 Quoted in John Leonard, "Why Not Use TV for a Head Start Program?" *New York Times Magazine*, July 14, 1968, pp. 24, 26.
27 Carolyn Brown, "McLuhan and the Dance," *Ballet Review* 1, no. 4 (1966):13.
28 Slavko Vorkapich, "Cine-Dance," *Dance Perspectives* 30 (Summer 1967): 43.
29 Vuillier, *A History of Dancing*, pp. 240–41.
30 Norman O. Brown, *Love's Body* (New York: Random House, 1968), p. 82.
31 Mary Wigman, *The Language of Dance*, trans. Walter Sorell (Middletown, Conn.: Wesleyan University Press, 1966), p. 12.
32 Susanne K. Langer, *Problems of Art* (New York: Scribner's, 1957), p. 11.
33 Ibid., p. 12.
34 Heinrich von Kleist, "Puppet Theatre," trans. Beryl De Zoete, in Beryl De Zoete, *The Thunder and the Freshness* (New York: Theatre Arts Books, 1963), pp. 70–71.

Perpetual Motions

1 Friedrich Nietzsche, *Thus Spoke Zarathustra*, trans. Walter Kaufmann (New York: Viking Press, 1966), p. 12.
2 W. Ehrenberg, "Maxwell's Demon," *Scientific American*, November 1967, p. 103. I have paraphrased Maxwell in these preceding two paragraphs.
3 Ibid., p. 109.
4 Jagjit Singh, *Great Ideas in Information Theory, Language and Cybernetics* (New York: Dover, 1966), p. 78. The phrase *certain vertigo* is Norbert Wiener's.
5 Thomas Pynchon, *The Crying of Lot 49* (New York: J. B. Lippincott, 1966), p. 131.
6 "Though [Pierce] had never talked business with her, she had known it to be a fraction of him that couldn't come out even, would carry forever beyond any decimal place she might name . . ." (ibid., p. 178).

There is a Chinese pi (so to speak) as well as a Greek. It is a jade disc, perfectly determinate, a symbol of heaven. The example in the Worcester (Mass.) Art Museum bears a relief carving of a dragon biting its tail.

7 Gaston Bachelard, *The Psychoanalysis of Fire*, trans. Alan C. M. Ross (Boston: Beacon Press, 1964), pp. 93–95.
8 Stanley W. Angrist, "Perpetual Motion Machines," *Scientific American*, January 1968, pp. 114–22.
9 Bachelard, *Psychoanalysis of Fire*, p. 56.
10 Roger Caillois, *Man, Play, and Games*, trans. Meyer Barash (New York: Free Press of Glencoe, 1961), p. 5. Caillois means games in which people consume (time, energy) but do not produce.

11 Vladimir Nabokov, *Invitation to a Beheading* (New York: Capricorn Books, 1965), p. 50.

12 Maxine Sheets, *The Phenomenology of Dance* (Madison: University of Wisconsin Press, 1966), p. 36.

13 Lynn White, *Medieval Technology and Social Change* (Oxford: Clarendon Press, 1966), p. 130. I have deleted the "perhaps" by which White qualifies "rooted."

14 Ananda Coomaraswamy, *The Dance of Shiva* (New York: Noonday Press, 1957), p. 76. Coomaraswamy is quoting the poet Tirumular.

15 Paul Valéry, "Philosophy of the Dance," in *Aesthetics*, trans. Ralph Manheim, vol. 13 of *Collected Works* (New York: Bollingen Foundation, 1964), p. 207.

16 Otto Mayr, "The Origins of Feedback Control," *Scientific American*, October 1970, p. 114.

17 Otto Mayr, "Adam Smith and the Concept of the Feedback System: Economic Thought and Technology in 18th-Century Britain," *Technology and Culture*, January 1971, p. 2.

18 Herman Melville, *Moby-Dick*, ed. Charles Feidelson, Jr. (Indianapolis: Bobbs-Merrill, 1964), pp. 23, 724.

19 Norbert Wiener, *The Human Use of Human Beings* (New York: Avon Books, 1967), p. 25.

20 Jane Austen, *Northanger Abbey* (New York: The New American Library, 1965), p. 510; *Persuasion* (New York: The New American Library, 1964), p. 104; *Sense and Sensibility* (Harmondsworth, England: Penguin Books, 1974), p. 74.

21 Charles Dickens, *Great Expectations* (New York: The New American Library, 1963), p. 56.

22 Philip Morrison and Emily Morrison, eds., *Charles Babbage and His Calculating Engines* (New York: Dover, 1961). Hugh Kenner has some fine observations on Babbage in *The Counterfeiters* (Bloomington: Indiana University Press, 1968), pp. 100–116, 143–58.

23 Quoted in H. P. Babbage, "The Analytical Engine," reprinted in Morrison and Morrison, *Charles Babbage*, p. 331.

24 Robert W. Daniel, Afterword to Anthony Trollope, *Barchester Towers* (New York: The New American Library, 1963), p. 531.

25 Conrad Hyers, *Zen and the Comic Spirit* (Philadelphia: The Westminster Press, 1973), p. 43.

26 T. S. Ashton, *The Industrial Revolution 1760–1830* (London: Oxford University Press, 1962), p. 70.

27 Basil Willey, *The Eighteenth-Century Background* (Boston: Beacon Press, 1961), p. 5.

28 Thomas Hardy, *Tess of the d'Urbervilles* (New York: W. W. Norton, 1965), pp. 269–72.

29 D. H. Lawrence, *The Rainbow* (New York: Viking Press, 1975), p. 448.

30 Ada Augusta, countess of Lovelace, "Notes by the Translator" (of the "Sketch of the Analytical Engine Invented by Charles Babbage" by L. F. Menebrea) in Morrison and Morrison, *Charles Babbage*, p. 284.

31 Joseph Conrad, *The Secret Agent* (Garden City, N.Y.: Doubleday, 1953), p. 66.

32 Ada Augusta, "Notes," p. 252.

33 M. I. Finley, *The World of Odysseus* (New York: Viking Press, 1954), p. 36.

34 Owen Barfield, *Saving the Appearances* (London: Faber and Faber, 1957), pp. 94–95.

35 Erwin Panofsky, *Early Netherlandish Painting* (New York: Harper and Row, 1971), 1:198.

36 Edmund Carpenter, *They Became What They Beheld* (New York: Outerbridge and Dienstfrey, 1970); see the section entitled "Avoidance of Stare."

37 Oliver Wendell Holmes, quoted in Beaumont Newhall, *The History of Photography* (New York: The Museum of Modern Art, 1964), p. 22.

38 Stanley Cavell, *The World Viewed* (New York: Viking Press, 1971), p. 23.

39 Vladimir Nabokov, "The Visit to the Museum," in *The Portable Nabokov*, ed. Page Stegner (New York: Viking Press, 1971), p. 111.

40 Gaston Bachelard, *The Poetics of Space*, trans. Maria Jolas (New York: The Orion Press, 1964), p. xi.

41 Stephen Marcus, "Freud and Dora," *Partisan Review* 41, no. 1 (1974): p. 92. Marcus mentions Dora's symptoms though not in their size places.

The Metamorphosis of Shit

1 The title of this essay derives from *The Metamorphosis of Ajax* (1596) (i.e., a jakes) by Sir John Harington. Harington reinvented the flush toilet (forgotten since Minoan times) and wrote a witty book in which, among other things, he described and illustrated his invention.

2 "A Panegyrick on the D[ea]n," in *The Poems of Jonathan Swift*, ed. Harold Williams, 3 Vols. (Oxford: Oxford University Press, 1958), 3:893.

Celia's biological being appals Strephon. In "The Lady's Dressing Room" (1730), astonished and undone, he repeats in "amorous Fits, / Oh! Celia, Celia, Celia shits." In "Strephon and Chloe" (1731), grown no wiser, he cries in astonishment: "ye Gods, what Sound is this? / Can Chloe, heav'nly Chloe [piss]?" But what absurdly appals one lover, absurdly delights another, Lady Chatterley's for instance: "An' if tha shits an' if tha pisses, I'm glad, I don't want a woman as couldna shit nor piss" (D. H. Lawrence, *Lady Chatterley's Lover* [New York: The New American Library, 1962], p. 208).

In the footrace in Book 23 of the *Iliad* Athena favors Odysseus, and Ajax, slipping in offal, finishes second. In the footrace in Book 2 of *The Dunciad*

Edmund Curll slips on an equally unpleasant surface, but now the goddess—not Athena but Cloacina, the selfsame gentle goddess of Swift's "Panegyrick"—heeds the prayer of her fallen votary. As Pope tells it, Curll rises to win the race, "Nor heeds the brown dishonours of his face" (*The Dunciad* in *Selected Poetry and Prose*, ed. William K. Wimsatt, Jr. [New York: Holt, Rinehart and Winston, 1965], p. 398).

3 Swift, of course, constructs a comic anthropology out of this vexation: "The very Moment [a Yahoo leader] is discarded, his Successor, at the Head of all the *Yahoos* in that District, Young and Old, Male and Female, come in a Body, and discharge their excrements upon him from Head to Foot" (*Gulliver's Travels* [New York: W. W. Norton, 1970], p. 228).

4 Northern Renaissance and post-Renaissance painting easily accommodates excremental imagery, for we find it not just in apocalyptic visions by Bosch, in satiric canards by Peter Brueghel the Elder and Peter van den Borch, in genre scenes by Adriaen van Ostade and Jan Miense Molenaer, in landscapes by Paulus Potter, but in biblical narratives by Rembrandt. For instance, in an etching of *The Good Samaritan*—an etching in which the Samaritan helps the injured man he has befriended—a dog squats and shits. Rembrandt (who on other occasions etched a man pissing, a woman pissing, and a couple making love) does not forget that God's plenty extends from the Christian to the creatural.

5 Luther, *Table Talk*, ed. Theodore G. Tappert and Helmut T. Lehmann; trans. Theodore G. Tappert (Philadelphia: Fortress, 1967), vol. 54 of *Luther's Works*, pp. 448, 83. Tappert translates *dreck* as stool, *arschloch* as anus.

6 Norman O. Brown, *Life Against Death* (New York: Random House, 1959), pp. 208–9.

7 Luther, *Letters I*, ed. Gottfried G. Krodel and Helmut T. Lehmann; trans. Gottfried G. Krodel (Philadelphia: Fortress, 1963), vol. 48 of *Luther's Works*, pp. 217, 291, 255.

8 Quoted in Lewis W. Spitz, "Psychohistory and History: The Case of *Young Man Luther*," in *Psychohistory and Religion*, ed. Roger A. Johnson (Philadelphia: Fortress, 1977), p. 79.

9 MS. no. 3232b, *Martin Luthers Werke, Tischreden*, 3 vols. (Weimar, 1967), as translated in Brown, *Life Against Death*, p. 202.

10 Luther, *Table Talk*, p. 193, n. 65.

11 W. H. Auden, "Greatness Finding Itself," in *Forewords and Afterwords* (New York: Random House, 1973), p. 86.

12 Erik Erikson, *Young Man Luther* (New York: Norton, 1962), p. 205.

13 Sandor Ferenczi, *Final Contributions to the Problems and Methods of Psycho-Analysis*, ed. Michael Balint; trans. Erich Mosbacher et al. (London: Hogarth Press and the Institute of Psycho-Analysis, 1955), p. 188.

14 Quoted in Albert E. Elsen, *Rodin* (London: Secker and Warburg, 1974), p. 52.

15 Peter Mathiessen, *The Snow Leopard* (New York: Viking Press, 1978), pp. 263–64.
16 Yevgeny Zamyatin, *We*, trans. Mirra Ginsburg (New York: Bantam Books, 1972), pp. 24, 166.
17 Aleksandr Zinoviev, *The Yawning Heights*, trans. Gordon Clough (New York: Random House, 1979), p. 29.
18 Ford Madox Ford, *The Good Soldier* (New York: Random House, 1955), p. 114.
19 James Joyce, *Ulysses* (New York: Random House, 1961), p. 69. Here, as elsewhere, further page references cited in this essay are to the text at hand.
20 Hélène Cixous, *The Exile of James Joyce*, trans. Sally A. J. Purcell (New York: D. Lewis, 1972), p. 727.
21 Ibid.
22 W. H. Auden, "The Geography of the House," in *About the House* (New York: Random House, 1965), p. 17. Writing graffiti in the toilet is an ur-act of literature, the literary equivalent of this "ur-act of making": at once expressive yet anonymous.
23 *Ulysses*, p. 68. Bloom reads a penny dreadful in the outhouse, but Henry Miller recommends the outhouse for reading certain passages in Rabelais, and—"if one wants to extract the full flavor of their content"—the toilet for certain passages in *Ulysses*. ("A Saturday Afternoon," in *Black Spring* [New York: Grove Press, 1963], pp. 42–43.)

Unlike Bloom's timid fantasy of authorship, So-and-So—the protagonist of Tommaso Landolfi's story, "The Death of the King of France"—indulges himself in megalomaniacal daydreams of knowledge and power atop a toilet seat. (*Gogol's Wife and Other Stories*, trans. Raymond Rosenthal, John Longrigg, Wayland Young [New York: New Directions, 1963], pp. 121–63.) The original title of Landolfi's story was "W.C."
24 David Levine drew a caricature of Jackson Pollock pissing the Drip Paintings into existence—in fact, Andy Warhol, impervious to satire, made several *Piss Paintings*—"urine on canvas" as the art historian would say—in the manner Levine deplored.
25 Peter Conrad, "Chewing Up the Soft Machine," *Times Literary Supplement*, May 30, 1980, p. 613.
26 J. K. Huysmans, *Against the Grain*, trans. from the French (New York: Dover, 1969), p. 195. Nevertheless, we want to speak cautiously of the aberrant enema. The ancient Mayans practiced anal ingestion of hallucinogens, having discovered that this procedure intoxicates very quickly and without nausea. The ancient Romans, on the other hand, practiced oral expulsion of chyme in the vomitorium. According to Ship Surgeon Gulliver (who ought to know) the sick Englishman repairs the inversion of Nature by inverting the uses of anus and mouth: "forcing Solids and Liquids in at the [former], and making Evacuations at the [latter]" (221).

The giant Pantagruel, Rabelais's sick Frenchman, evacuates at the mouth without benefit of theory. Laxatives having failed, he swallows seventeen hollow balls, each with a man inside. These men break down a great constipated mound in his stomach, the fragments of which they load into baskets and pack into the balls. Pantagruel vomits the lot, and, in this grotesque variant of Jonah's rebirth, restores himself to health.

If taking an enema is a decadent way of being fed, perhaps reading a book is a decadent way of being moved. Or as Mark Twain rather brutally joked: if you really want to be moved, don't read a book, take an enema. (Alan Spiegel, "American Film-Flam," *Salmagundi* 41 [Spring 1978]: 169.)

27 The Marquis de Sade, *The 120 Days of Sodom*, trans. Austryn Wainhouse and Richard Seaver (New York: Grove Press, 1966), p. 520.

28 François Rabelais, *The Histories of Gargantua and Pantagruel*, trans. J. M. Cohen (Harmondsworth, England: Penguin Books, 1976), p. 69.

29 Emile Zola, *L'Assommoir*, trans. Leonard Tancock (Harmondsworth, England: Penguin Books, 1976), p. 330.

30 Juan Goytisolo, *Juan the Landless*, trans. Helen R. Lane (New York: Viking Press, 1977), p. 10.

31 There is, to be sure, a semantic identity of hidden face with face—nether eye with eye, nether cheek with cheek—though poor Absalon's confusion of them in *The Miller's Tale* is certainly not semantic. There is also a direct physiological reciprocity between the opened trachea and closed anus (while eating), the opened anus and closed trachea (while shitting), and there are many metaphors of physiological similitude: for example, farting and sneezing (in Kenneth Burke's analysis of the "Pig and Pepper" episode in *Alice in Wonderland*), farting and whispering (in Swift's verse-riddle "Because I am by Nature blind"), farting and speaking *and* eating (in the asshole's bureaucratization of the body in Burroughs's *Naked Lunch*), farting and carrying a tune (in the actual stage performances of the French virtuoso Joseph Pujol), farting and music making (in Mozart's use of those "explosions of air from brass instruments in a comic sense unmistakeably parallel to [the scatological playfulness of] his comic letters") (Bridget Brophy, *Mozart the Dramatist* [New York: Harcourt, Brace and World, 1964], p. 254).

In *Humphry Clinker* Smollett associates excreting with confession: "Frogmore [was] enthroned on an easing-chair, under the pressure of a double evacuation. The short intervals betwixt every heave he employed in crying for mercy, confessing his sins, or asking the vicar's opinion of his case . . ." (Tobias Smollett, *Humphry Clinker* [New York: New American Library, 1960], p. 302).

32 Günter Grass, *The Flounder*, trans. Ralph Manheim (New York: Harcourt Brace Jovanovich, 1978), p. 237.

33 Kurt Vonnegut, *Slaughter-House Five* (New York: Delacorte Press, 1969), p. 109.

34 Carlo Levi, *Christ Stopped at Eboli*, trans. Frances Frenaye (New York: Farrar, Straus, 1976), p. 96.

35 Lawrence Wright, *Clean and Decent* (London: Routledge and Kegan Paul, 1980), p. 73. The wittiest closestool I know of—middle-class French, c. 1675—draws an immediate connection between reading and shitting. This stool, which might have fooled even Strephon, is disguised as a multivolume pile of books whose title—in allusion to the Franco-Dutch wars—is *Voyage au Pays Bas* ("Voyage to the Low Country"). See ibid., p. 74, for an illustration.

"Books [in fact] and other printed matter are a curious symbol of feces," according to Ernest Jones, "presumably through the association with paper and the idea of pressing (smearing, imprinting)" ("Anal Erotic Character Traits," in *Papers on Psycho-Analysis* [Baltimore: W. Wood, 1938], p. 543). The truest realization of printed matter as shit is paper money. "Toilet paper, banknote stock, [and] newsprint," observes Thomas Pynchon, are "a medium or ground for shit, money and the Word" (*Gravity's Rainbow* [New York: Bantam Books, 1980], p. 31). Toilet paper cleans the human body. Banknote stock mirrors the world's body. Newsprint informs the body politic.

36 Freud, *Civilization and Its Discontents* (London: Hogarth, 1961), vol. 21 of *The Complete Psychological Works of Sigmund Freud*, trans. James Strachey (1953–1974), pp. 99–100. Freud's principal essays on anality are "Character and Anal Erotism," in *Works* (London, 1959), 9:169–75, and "On Transformations of Instinct as Exemplified in Anal Erotism," in *Works* (London, 1955), 17:127–33.

37 Ferenczi, "The Ontogenesis of the Interest in Money," in *Sex in Psycho-Analysis*, trans. Ernest Jones (New York: Dover, 1958), pp. 269–79. "The delight in gold and in the possession of money ["the capitalistic instinct"] represents anal-erotism" (279). Yahoos, however, are unrepressed anal-erotics *and* instinctive capitalists: they are "violently fond" of certain shining stones which they hoard in their kennels (226–27).

38 Mary Douglas, "Pollution," in the *International Encyclopedia of the Social Sciences*, ed. David L. Sills (New York: Macmillan, 1968–1979), 12:336–41. See also Christian Enzensberger, *Smut*, trans. Sandra Morris (New York: The Seabury Press, 1974).

39 Ved Mehta, "Mahatma Gandhi and His Apostles," *New Yorker*, May 10, 1976, p. 52.

40 Antonin Artaud, *Selected Writings*, ed. Susan Sontag; trans. Helen Weaver (New York: Farrar, Straus and Giroux, 1976), p. 453.

41 Laurence Sterne, *The Life and Opinions of Tristram Shandy, Gentleman* (Boston: Houghton Mifflin, 1965), p. 225.

42 Aristotle's *Theory of Poetry and Fine Art*, trans. S. H. Butcher (New York:

Dover, 1951), p. 225. See also Kenneth Burke, "On Catharsis, or Resolution," *Kenyon Review* 16 (Summer 1959):337–75.

43 *The Comedy of Dante Alighieri*, trans. Dorothy Sayers (New York: Basic Books, 1962), 1:287.

44 As Vergil and Dante are reborn anally from the ice-bound Devil at the center of the Earth, Spring is reborn from the ice-bound earth of Winter in *Walden*: in a manner, says Thoreau, which "is somewhat excrementitious in its character, and there is no end to the heaps of liver, lights, and bowels . . ." (*Walden* [New York: Random House, 1950], p. 275.). These rebirths are parthenogenetic, like a child's fantasy of anal birth.

45 Jae Num Lee, *Swift and Scatological Satire* (Albuquerque: University of New Mexico Press, 1971), p. 18. In *Martin Chuzzlewit* Dickens echoes Dante's description of Hell in his description of Eden, a noxious village on the American frontier: the air is fetid, the earth miry, the forest putrescent. Offal everywhere.

46 Herman Melville, *The Confidence-Man* (New York: Grove Press, 1955), p. 293.

47 Gustave Flaubert, *Bouvard and Pécuchet*, trans. A. J. Krailsheimer (Harmondsworth, England: Penguin Books, 1976), p. 286.

48 Jean-Paul Sartre, *Nausea*, trans. Lloyd Alexander (New York: New Directions, 1964), p. 131.

49 Terrence Des Pres, *The Survivor* (New York: Oxford University Press, 1976), pp. 51–71.

50 Louis-Ferdinand Céline, *Death on the Installment Plan*, trans. Ralph Manheim (New York: New Directions, 1966), pp. 397, 396.

51 Charles Baudelaire, "On the Essence of Laughter," trans. Jonathan Mayne, in *Comedy: Meaning and Form*, ed. Robert W. Corrigan (San Francisco: Chandler, 1965), p. 451.

52 Bertolt Brecht, *Edward II*, English version by Eric Bentley (New York: Grove Press, 1966), p. 87.

53 Carlyle said of *Sartor Resartus*: "I do sometimes think the book *will* prove a kind of medicinal *assafoetida* [i.e., emetic] for the pudding stomach of England, and produce new secretions there" (notes to *Sartor Resartus*, ed. Archibald MacMechan [Boston: Ginn, 1925], p. 282). Compare Marcel Duchamp on Dada: It "was very serviceable as a purgative. And I think I was thoroughly conscious of this at the time and of a desire to effect a purgation in myself " (*Dadas on Art*, ed. J. J. Sweeney [Englewood Cliffs, N.J.: Prentice-Hall, 1971], p. 141).

The *Fountain* is comically obscene, and it offended its first audience (the exhibitors who refused to exhibit it). But comic obscenity is hardly excremental assault, and Duchamp is not Alfred Jarry, the first modern artist to usher scatology into a public place. The first word of *Ubu Roi* (1896) is

"Merdre!" [*sic*]—an exclamation that not only sets the tone of the play that follows but that precipitated a free-for-all among its first auditors.

54 *Molloy*, trans. Patrick Bowles and Samuel Beckett in *Three Novels of Samuel Beckett* (New York: Grove Press, 1965), p. 16. Murphy's last wish is a last taste of the shit: that the cremated remains of his body, mind, and soul be flushed away in a "necessary house" of the Abbey Theatre. Beckett, *Murphy* (New York: Grove Press, 1982), p. 269.

55 Sexual and excretory functions share a common passage in various animals, but even in human beings (where these passages only partially coincide) erotic anality is not uncommon in adults. It is perhaps not beside the point that in *Maurice*, E. M. Forster's novel of homosexual love, Maurice empties sick Clive's chamber pot, claiming it's the sort of thing lovers do for one another. Doubtless Maurice would not want a man as couldna shit nor piss, but lovers never empty one another's chamber pot in Forster's novels of heterosexual love.

56 *Malone Dies* in *Three Novels of Samuel Beckett*, p. 283.

57 Beckett, *Molloy*, p. 116.

58 Albert T. Simeons, *Man's Presumptuous Brain* (New York: Dutton, 1962), p. 89. I draw the example of the deer in the glade from Simeons.

59 For a thoroughgoing analysis of obscenity in Aristophanes, see Jeffrey Henderson, *The Maculate Muse: Obscene Language in Attic Comedy* (New Haven: Yale University Press, 1975).

60 Ernest Hemingway, *In Our Time* (New York: Scribner's, 1958), p. 193.

61 Theodore Reik, *The Unknown Murderer*, trans. Katherine Jones (New York: International Universities Press, 1949), pp. 76–81.

62 Jean Genet, *The Thief's Journal*, trans. Bernard Frechtman (New York: Bantam Books, 1965), p. 203.

63 Norman Mailer, "The Metaphysics of the Belly," in *The Presidential Papers* (New York: G. P. Putnam's Sons, 1963), p. 291.

64 On his third voyage Gulliver meets a professor at the Academy of Lagado who advises "great statesmen" on how to uncover plots and conspiracies against the government: ascertain the diet of the suspects, when they eat, on which side they sleep, and "with which Hand they wiped their Posteriors." Furthermore, "take a strict View of their Excrements, and from the Colour, the Odour, the Taste, the Consistence, the Crudeness, or Maturity of Digestion, form a Judgment of their Thoughts and Designs." For, after all, argues this professor—here is the part about self and cellular knowledge—"when he used merely as a Trial to consider which was the best Way of murdering the King, his Ordure would have a Tincture of Green; but quite different when he thought only of raising an insurrection, or burning the Metropolis" (162–63).

65 William Gass, review of *Genius and Lust*, ed. Norman Mailer, *New York Times Book Review*, October 24, 1976, p. 2.

66 Antoinette Dauber, "Herrick's Foul Epigrams," *Genre* 9 (Summer 1976): 87–102.

The Museum, My Home Away From Home

1 Linda Nochlin, "Museums and Radicals: A History of Emergencies," in *Museums in Crisis*, ed. Brian O'Doherty (New York: George Braziller, 1972), p. 32. Less awestruck observers associate the museum with less awe-inspiring images. Nelson Goodman has made a handy, "not altogether facetious," list: jailhouse, madhouse, teahouse, ball park, hospital, library. See "The End of the Museum?" *New Criterion* 2 (October 1983):9.

2 The museum has often enough been defined as a necropolis and cemetery. Nochlin, "Museums and Radicals," cites Pissarro and Marinetti respectively (pp. 22, 23). The "old-age home" is her revision of a remark by Etienne Gilson (p. 39 n. 40). Hugh Kenner's witty essay in *Museums in Crisis* is entitled "Epilogue: The Dead-Letter Office," pp. 161–74.

3 Nochlin, "Museums and Radicals," p. 22.

4 Quoted in Karl E. Meyer, *The Art Museum* (New York: Morrow, 1979), p. 42.

Q. Should a cultural complex (if not a museum) be a public playground?

A. Yes, if the playground is the Beaubourg in Paris, a French version of American Pop art.

Q. Should a cultural complex be a formal garden?

A. No, if the garden is Lincoln Center in New York, a concrete version of French Neo-Classicism.

5 "Without any categories at all we are helpless and confused," writes E. H. Gombrich proposing "to speak as a person who goes to museums because he likes looking at works of art" but who sounds suspiciously like an art historian. See "The Museum: Past, Present and Future," in *Ideals and Idols* (Oxford: Phaidon, 1979), pp. 200, 189.

6 Kenneth Hudson, *A Social History of Museums* (Atlantic Highlands, N.J.: Humanities Press, 1975), p. 53.

7 Nochlin, "Museums and Radicals," p. 25.

8 Eugenio Donato quoted in Douglas Crimp, "On the Museum's Ruins," *October* 13 (Summer 1980):49–50.

9 Gustave Flaubert, *Bouvard and Pécuchet*, trans. A. J. Krailsheimer (Harmondsworth, England: Penguin Books, 1976), p. 103.

10 See Crimp "On the Museum's Ruins," p. 56.

11 Flaubert, *Bouvard and Pécuchet*, p. 48.

Sources for Illustrations

1 Emanuele Anati, *Camonica Valley*, trans. from the French by Linda Asher (New York: Knopf, 1961), p. 217.

2 Charles Barsotti, *New York Times*, August 19, 1973, sect. 4, p. 15. President Nixon takes refuge. Copyright © 1973 by The New York Times Co. Reprinted by permission.

3, 4, 5 The bent nails, as drawn by the author, in various postures of entanglement and disentanglement.

6 Edgar Allan Poe, *The Narrative of Arthur Gordon Pym*. The two triangles represent wells eastward of the third chasm.

7 The Philadelphia Museum of Art

8 W. H. Matthews, *Mazes and Labyrinths* (New York: Dover Publications, 1970), p. 46.

9 *Buffalo Evening News*, November 17, 1973, comics section. Reprinted by permission of Rath Packing Company.

10 G. R. Levy, *The Gate of Horn* (London: Faber and Faber, 1948), p. 12.

11 John Layard, "Maze-Dances and the Ritual of the Labyrinth in Malekula," *Folk-Lore* 47 (June 1936): 139.

12 W. H. Matthews, *Mazes and Labyrinths* (New York: Dover Publications, 1970), p. 58.

13 W. H. Matthews, *Mazes and Labyrinths* (New York: Dover Publications, 1970), p. 64.

14 Jagjit Singh, *Great Ideas in Information Theory, Language and Cybernetics* (New York: Dover Publications, 1966), p. 76.

15 *McGraw-Hill Encyclopedia of Science and Technology* (New York, 1960), 10:35.
16 The Museum of Modern Art (New York)
17 Otto Mayr, "The Origins of Feedback Control," *Scientific American*, October 1970, p. 114. I have paraphrased Mayr in the caption.
18 *Funk and Wagnall's Standard College Dictionary* (New York, 1963), p. 579.
19 K. G. Pontus Hultén, *The Machine* (New York: The Museum of Modern Art, 1968), p. 155.
20 The Philadelphia Museum of Art
21 The National Gallery (London). Reproduced by courtesy of the Trustees.
22 Staatliche Kunstsammlungen, Dresden
23 Erle Loran, *Cézanne's Composition* (Berkeley: University of California Press, 1946), p. 20.
24 The Philadelphia Museum of Art
25 The British Museum (London). Reprinted with permission of the Trustees.
26, 27 Lucinda Lambton, *Temples of Convenience* (New York: St. Martin's Press, 1978), figs. 24 and 25. A late eighteenth- or early nineteenth-century English cabinet with chamber pot, opened and closed.
28 *Illusions*, ed. Edi Lanners, trans. Heinz Norden (New York: Holt, Rinehart and Winston, 1973), p. 53.
29 The Philadelphia Museum of Art
30 Manzoni printed each label in four languages—Italian, German, French, and English—as if he were an international manufacturer of household products. There is a photo of him standing in a bathroom, smiling broadly, displaying one of his tins. Manzoni filled ninety of them and pegged the price of shit to the daily price of gold.
31 Sidney Janis Gallery (New York)
32 Lucinda Lambton, *Temples of Convenience* (New York: St. Martin's Press, 1978), fig. 15. A royal closestool, seventeenth-century English. My caption paraphrases hers.
33 Lucinda Lambton, *Temples of Convenience* (New York: St. Martin's Press), fig. 57.
34 Hilton Hotel (Tokyo). Courtesy of Jan Gordon.
35 St. Petronius (Bologna)

Index of Names and Titles

References to illustrations are italicized and follow other references.